RECALLING THE PAST

...WHILE I STILL CAN

GERARD GRANT

FOREWORD BY BESTSELLING SCOTTISH
AUTHOR ANNA SMITH

Contents

Frightening dreams

This book is dedicated to my family.

"Rejoice with your family in the beautiful land of life!"
– Albert Einstein

FOREWORD

Most of us grew up listening to the stories of our parents. They painted a picture so that the world they lived in long before we were born would not be lost to us.

It was a greater gift they gave us than we probably realised as we sat mesmerised by the tales they weaved of their own childhood, stories of big families, of hardship and relationships.

Because of them, we had an insight into their lives that no amount of schooling or education could truly give us.

Storytelling is an art, and it is the legacy our parents and grandparents bestowed on us. And Gerard Grant's stories, here in this collection, make sure that this history of where we came from will be there for our children and grandchildren.

With his ability to tell the story, Gerard brings to life so many snapshots of characters and events as he grew up in Calderbank and the surrounding villages. From the miners to the neighbours to the parish priests, it is a vivid picture of a bygone era.

I loved every minute of it. And especially when Gerard takes us on his own travels – an innocent young teenager abroad, soaking up all the sights where every day another tale unfolded.

But this book is more than a raft of anecdotes. It is part of our history, of our heritage, and I thank Gerard for taking the time to sit down and leave us with this collection of gems to treasure.

Anna Smith

PREFACE

The catalyst to start writing this book of memories was when one of my daughters, Maureen, gave me a little booklet in which I had to handwrite answers to a number of questions. It was entitled 'Questions I asked my Dad' and posed questions like… What was the house that you first lived in like? Where did you spend your holidays as a child? How did you meet my Mum? What was your first job?

This hardbacked booklet measured only about 5inches x 5inches and had only one page allocated to each question. As it had to be completed in my best handwriting and I would want to elaborate on some of the answers, I knew the small page would have insufficient space. So, I first set the questions and answers on a word document on my computer to enable me to edit it and be sure that my answers could be contained within a page before I actually started to write.

Having done that, I was quite pleased with the booklet and thought that my other three children and indeed my six grandchildren would also like to own a copy of the book. As I had all the text done, I included some appropriate photos and it was an easy task to print it and produce a dozen copies of a neat little booklet, which indeed was greatly appreciated by all of them.

I had always promised myself that someday I would 'write my book' and that little booklet was in fact the beginning… a start was made!

So, whom must I thank for their assistance, inspiration and endurance in the production of this book?

I think firstly I must thank God for the life I have been blessed with, the health and wealth He bestowed on me and the wonderful wife He gave me. I say He gave me, because Rena was fully intent on serving God as a nun before she met me. So, Thank You God again for my wife Rena, our four incredible children and six grandchildren and the great grandchildren that have now started to appear on this earth.

I must also thank my brother Joe and sister Mary Therese who occasionally reminded me and clarified or confirmed many points or events mentioned in the book.

Great credit also must go to my two internet friends, Mr Google and Mr Wikipedia. Many items mentioned herein were confirmed and embellished by researching and calling on their unlimited knowledge. My daughter Maureen, with her experience of teaching English to young children in Abu Dhabi with the British Council, was the ideal person to edit the text. Her pro bono offer could not be rejected.

My grandson Scott, a genius on computers, graphics and countless other talents was adamant that he be responsible for preparing the book for publication. He provided many tips on how I should put everything together and he also designed the front and back cover. Thank you Scott.

My artistic grandson Connor produced a hand drawn portrait of me, which I felt was a perfect choice for the front cover of the book.

Thanks too to my son-in-law Colin, for his expert photography and he is my 'go to man' for anything relating to computers.

I wish to thank Google Images for any photographs and graphics I have reproduced and similarly The Airdrie & Coatbridge Advertiser for a reproduction of a photograph from their publication.

Also to any member of my extended family for giving me permission to use their photograph, plus, of course, anyone whom I have forgotten and with my memory, it's very possible there are a few.

As one gets older one's memory deteriorates so I thought I'd better get things down on paper whilst I still CAN remember, hence the title 'Recalling the Past... While I Still Can'

So, the stories in this book are just some memories of things I've done or experienced, descriptions of how I recall events or how things were or looked like in my mind. It is not in any kind of chronological order and I jump from childhood to adulthood and back at random. Memories are like that, you can be thinking of your teenage years one minute and you are in your forties the next.

Perhaps even some readers will connect and resonate with some of the recollections in their own lives and maybe some Airdrionians of my generation may also recall some names and places.

Memories are greatly enhanced by music and song. I get all sentimental when I hear songs of the 50s by Frank Sinatra, Dean Martin, Perry Como, Bing Crosby, Ella Fitzgerald, Nat 'King' Cole, Connie Francis, Doris Day, Pat Boone and countless other 'real singers'. Their songs had lyrics that were decipherable, they were sung at a slower pace, providing laid back, easy listening.

I really believe that the songs and music you hear between the ages of 15 and 21 will live forever in your memory as your 'all time greats'. When you hear these classics, all too rarely now I add, it brings a smile and jogs a memory of many very happy times.

Ah nostalgia is a great thing. Nostalgia? … that's a thing of the past is it not?

HIGH STREET AIRDRIE

Airdrie House was a very old mansion and the date of construction is unclear but some reports state that one of the original owners was a brother-in-law to the Scottish hero William Wallace. It is also believed that Wallace and his troops camped there before the Battle of Falkirk in 1298. This was one of the major battles in the First War of Scottish Independence. Wallace was defeated in that battle by King Edward I of England.

Now this is not the opening chapter in a historical lesson, I just mention these facts because Airdrie House was where I was born in 1938. It was known then as Airdrie House Maternity Home and was situated approximately where the Monklands Hospital now stands.

Sir John Wilson, who acquired the estate, bequeathed it to the Burgh of Airdrie on his death in 1918 and the mansion became the maternity home until it closed in 1962 to make way for the building of the Hospital.

I had often wondered, when I went dancing at Airdrie Palais in The *Sir John Wilson Town Hall*, just who this 'John Wilson' was.

I now know that he was a successful businessman and local politician and the benefactor who ensured that the town of Airdrie benefitted

1

from the West End Park and the Centenary Park as well as the impos-ing Town Hall.

There is no plaque on the new hospital building to commemorate my birthplace, I don't expect there ever will be, as I have not done an-ything to warrant such accolade, nor have I been guilty of any infa-mous act.

I was the last-born child into a family of seven children, although Hugh Francis who would have been my oldest brother lived for only nine months. All my other siblings lived into retirement age at least.

Our home was an upstairs two bedroom flat in High Street in Airdrie, entered by an outside, open, concrete staircase. Our neighbour, who had three children, shared the open top landing. She was a widow, her husband a casualty of the war. I was born just prior to the outbreak of war in 1939 but don't accept any responsibility for war being de-clared! We were considered fortunate in that we had a small inside toilet that was reached through our small scullery then descended two steps down. I believe this toilet actually was once shared with our neighbour, and previously we would have been required to go out our front door to enter it from the outside staircase before the entry was made from our scullery.

A new construction on to our neighbour's house and their downstairs neighbour provided them with their own inside toilet. Perhaps their newly constructed facility had a small washbasin, I was never inside to see, but on second thoughts no, it probably did not, as that would have been considered an unnecessary luxury in the 1920s.

Through the main door of the house and then through the half glass door led to the long lobby, a lobby that was a favourite 'field' for all sorts of ball games when it was raining outside.

On the left was a small bedroom with a fireplace and further down the lobby on the left was a 'lobby press'. 'Press' was the common name for a cupboard or small storage space. This press measured about 5ft by 4ft. Apart from containing the electric meter high on the wall, this cupboard, to use the modern term, provided substantial storage space. My memory of it however, is it being crammed full of stuff, mainly coats and all kinds of old clothing piled on top of one another.

It was always difficult to close the door and hold everything inside and there were always lots of empty beer bottles, evidence of my father's addiction. The reason these bottles weren't just thrown out was because there was a 2pence deposit on beer bottles if you could get the pubs to take them back. Many times I went round the 'family departments' of the pubs trying to earn some money returning the bottles, but mostly in vain. "Naw, yer daddy didnae get them here son" was the usual response.

So, to get back to the lobby press… to reach the prepaid electric meter and insert the penny I would have to climb up on to the 'stuff', precariously balance long enough to insert the penny or two to provide a further supply of power for the lights.

Electric lights, of course, was the only use we had for the electricity supply in our upstairs flat. Heating was by coal fire, cooking was either by a gas stove or the open fire. The wireless worked off an accumulator battery (I'll get back to accumulators shortly), there was no electric iron or kettle or any other electrical appliance, so light bulbs was the only use of electricity, a few pennies in the meter would last quite some time… oh for the good old days!

We had one very big front bedroom with windows on to High Street. It also had a 'press' and the thing I remember most being kept in that cupboard, was my Mickey Mouse gas mask. These were issued to every child during the war.

The main living room was quite large it had an old black lead range, which provided heating in the house and could also be used for cooking and baking. There was a tall mantelpiece above it and I could only reach it if I stood on a chair. This fireplace of course was very dirty and stoury and the chimney needed swept occasionally or it could catch fire. That was a very common occurrence as all houses in those days had open fires so when we heard the fire engine bells it was most likely responding to a chimney fire.

Cleaning the range was a dirty job. The black cast iron had to be scrubbed with 'Black Lead' to give it a clean and a shine. The silvery trim had to be cleaned with 'Silvo', a sort of silver polish cleaner. Cleaning and polishing the fire range was almost a full days work if done properly.

Within this living room, which, by the way, was never called the living room or the lounge, it was always called the 'kitchen', we had two recessed double beds which slept the four boys.

So you had three walls around each bed and therefore no ability to walk around it. This made it a bit tricky to make up the bed and I always remember my granny used a walking stick to spread the sheets and blankets in the bed recesses in her flat.

These beds were quite high off the floor, probably over 3ft. high. A rod holding a curtain screwed into the board at the front of the bed hid the space under the bed. This was referred to as the 'bed pawn'. I didn't know whether the 'pawn' referred to the curtain or the space under the bed, but my sister Mary Therese confirmed it was what we called the curtain. Anyway, this huge space under each bed was used also for storage, a dumping ground for everything and anything that could be shoved under. I could spend ages under the bed looking for things but I was always fearful of encountering a mouse. Yes we had lots of mice in the house. We had cats from time to time but they didn't earn their keep in ridding us of the mice (I'll get back to cats later).

The only other items in the 'kitchen' were a table and a few chairs, two couches, a sideboard with drawers below and mirrors and shelves above. This sideboard was situated adjacent to a large window that gave us a clear view of the Airdrie town clock so we depended on that timepiece for the precise time rather than our large wall clock, which occasionally, may not have been wound up and gave the wrong time.

I mention Airdrie town clock and it's tall green steeple because that iconic building represented home to me.

My first spell of being away from home was when I was doing my National Service and when I thought of home, I would get a picture in my mind of Airdrie town clock. When I was actually physically seeing it, then I knew I was truly back home, so that green top of the steeple meant a lot to me.

Continuing with the 'kitchen' contents... we had a wireless, that's what we called the radio and it worked from an accumulator battery. (I still occasionally call the radio a wireless even though my children and grandchildren ridicule me for it, old habits die hard).

There was a free-standing, tall wooden press that contained all the foodstuffs and potatoes. That was our pantry but we never called it such. The bottom shelf had a bucket of coal and bunches of firewood for kindling the fire. This was situated next to the small narrow scullery. The main stock of coal was in a coal cellar underneath the outside staircase, so going outside in cold and wet weather to fill a pail of coal was a bit of a pain and a heavy haul up the stairs for a wee thin laddie like me.

The scullery dimensions were probably about 5ft wide by about 7ft long and on the left wall there was an old cooker then the double sink. The double sink in the scullery had only one water tap, cold water of course and the only water supply in the house. When we required hot water for any purpose, dish washing for example or shaving, we had to boil a kettle on the gas hob.

At the edge of the sink there would be a bar of carbolic soap on a soap-dish, and a glass holding the toothbrushes. Toothpaste today comes in plastic tubes but it was very common in 1940s for it to come in a small tin about 2inches in diameter and about half inch deep. There was one brand that I recall - Gibbs SR Toothpaste - it was a solid pink coloured block. You wet your toothbrush and scrubbed it on the hard block of cleaning material. Everyone in the household would be using this same tin so it would not be considered very hygienic by today's standards.

On the opposite wall of the scullery there was only room for an orange box that we utilised to store our pots and pans. When I say 'orange' box I don't mean the colour of it. Fruit shops received their oranges in thin wooden boxes about 15"x30"x12" and separated into two compartments. When this stood on its end it gave you a wee unit with a shelf and all our pots were stored there. Above it on that wall was the gas meter, which also was fed by pennies to supply the gas.

Every now and then the 'gas man' would come and empty the meter. He would deposit the pennies on the kitchen table and start counting the total. We always got a small amount returned after he calculated the cost of how much gas we used. It wasn't much money so the refunded pennies usually went back into the meter. Sometimes I would manage to snaffle a few for a bar of toffee.

The door next to the sink led in to the toilet. We were fortunate that we no longer required to go outside onto the staircase to enter this toilet. It was however, not ideal, nor hygienic that the toilet was really just an extension of the scullery.

The backcourt and drying green was common to all four of the houses through our close and the outside washhouse was also shared. Each household was allocated a specific day for 'your day in the wash-house' and that was a full days work.

Inside the brick built washhouse there was a wooden low table to hold your large zinc 'washing byne' (these were also used for baths inside the house). There was a double sink, a wringer, and of course, water supply to the sink.

About a quarter of the space in the washhouse was taken up with the very large brick built boiler, which was filled by extending a hose from the sink. The water had then to be boiled by the coal fire under the boiler, so lighting the fire and filling the boiler was the first step. It took quite a while for the large quantity of water to come to the boil and the fire would require more coal added as required, to ensure the water stayed warm.

Soap flakes were added to give you soapy water and then the washing begun. The whites and linens would be done first followed by shirts and trousers and the dirty working clothes were last. Clothes would be moved around and lifted out using large wooden tongs and put in the sink.

To make sure they were clean they were rubbed on a washboard and rubbed with a bar of 'Sunlight' or 'Fairy' washing soap. All this was quite hard work, and they were then rinsed in the cold water before they were put through the wringer.

You hoped that your allocated washday was not a rainy one. The washing was then pinned to the ropes on the common drying green and a clothes pole used to hold the rope high up. This was the process with each category of the washing and the water in the boiler got dirt-ier with each batch of clothes. That's why the whites were done first.

Nevertheless there were occasions when a neighbour would say "Don't run your hot water away, I've a few things I'd like tae get washed when your finished".

No one today, would dream of using someone else's second hand water in which to wash their clothes… ugh!

The aforementioned large zinc washing byne was used to give me a bath in front of the fire in 'the kitchen'. I suppose it was used for bathing my other brothers and sisters too when they were younger but my nearest sibling was my brother Jim and he was four years my senior so I can only remember seeing him being bathed in the byne and not the older ones.

My earnest desire in the first twelve years of my life was to live in a house with an inside toilet and a bath. That was a dream. I yearned for a new council house but there was a massive waiting list after the war for a council house.

Showers were not common in houses in those days and the only place we got showers was at Airdrie Public Baths. That was the name above the entrance, it wasn't called Airdrie Swimming Pool as one would expect as we went there basically for swimming. Showering was just part of the process and we used the very strong smelling red carbolic soap provided. I loved the smell of carbolic soap, it meant cleanliness to me, and I still love the smell of carbolic soap even though I very rarely come across it now.

ANDERSON SHELTERS

During the war there were many air raid shelters built. The council houses around us in West Kirk Street and elsewhere had 'Anderson Shelters' erected in their gardens. Anderson Shelters were constructed from six corrugated iron sheets bolted together with steel plates at either end. They were small only 6ft 6in x 4ft 6in and had two bench seats. They were half submerged in the ground and then covered over with earth and grass.

When the air raid sirens were sounded the families were supposed to move into the shelters where they would be safe from falling rubble. That was the theory anyway. They were used after the war as garden huts, kids dens and storage huts. Our gang often played cards in some of them and probably some other unmentionable activities took place therein.

We, in the flats, did not have these shelters and our 'close' was designated as our air raid shelter. At either end of the close there was a very thick felt curtain, one side of which was a kind of leatherette material. On one side there were fold down bench seats the full length of the close. I only remember hearing the sirens and going down to the close on one occasion, perhaps there were more but I was too young to remember. The German bombers were targeting the Clydebank shipyards rather than Airdrie, but no doubt there were a few occasions when the pilots got a bit lost.

At the mouth of our close and most other closes in the street they built brick baffle walls at the kerb of the pavement. They were about 7ft high x 6ft wide x 2ft thick and were intended to protect us from a blast entering the close.

During the war the 'blackout' rules meant there were to be no lights visible at night, no street lamps and everyone had to have blackout blinds on their windows. So if there was no moonlight or it was cloudy you were walking in pitch darkness.

Needless to say many people bumped into these baffle walls in the dark and I remember bumping into them when running in the street. I was almost knocked unconscious one time and had a huge bump on my brow. I think in our town at least, there were many more injuries attributed to baffle walls than those caused by bombing.

On the spare ground at the top of the Wellwynd there were two or three large air raid shelters built with bricks or concrete. They were half submerged and totally covered in earth and grass so they just looked like small hills, they were very much bigger than the Anderson Shelters and were intended for a greater number of people.

After the war we regularly played cowboys and Indians on these 'hills'. There were a few steps down to enter the shelters to bring you on to floor level inside but they were, by this time, in a state of neglect and there were dangerous broken pieces of reinforced concrete with the steel reinforcement wires protruding from the broken concrete lying about the entrance.

If you were 'shot' during the cowboy and Indian battle you simulated the action and rolled over clasping the wound. There were no Hollywood casting agents watching you but you played the part as though there was.

I remember the day my brother Joe got 'shot', he rolled over and actually fell down into the entrance area. A protruding wire in the concrete made a huge gash in his leg. This was indeed a serious accident, blood everywhere, and it required I think about 15 stitches. For the remainder of his life he had a scar about four inches long and half an inch wide, kind of banana shape.

I also have a similar scar on the left leg too but less than half the size of Joe's. I had been walking in the bedroom on my hands with feet up in the air. My legs fell over and the left one came sharply against the wooden bedstead which was chamfered at the top edge making it as sharp as a knife. That scar also stayed with me throughout my life.

THE WIRELESS

Now, I don't suppose many of the younger generation will know what a wireless accumulator was.

Before radios were powered by electricity, the source of power for the 'Wireless' valves was an accumulator. An accumulator was a large lead-acid rechargeable battery in a glass container.

Wires led from the positive and negative points of the accumulator to the wireless. I wondered why, if it had wires, did they call it a 'wire-LESS' surely a contradiction of terms.

From memory, the accumulator we had probably only measured about 6 or 7 inches square by about 9 or 10 inches high but at five or six years of age they looked much bigger and to me they weighed a ton. Through the glass it just looked like it was filled with water. I was always told to be careful not to drop it and break the glass when I was taking it to be recharged. They said the acid would burn me.

I also was told that sometimes a child being sent to recharge the accumulator would be warned not to swing it around when carrying it… "If ye swing it around, ye'll mix up the stations and we'll no be able to get the light programme".

I only remember the BBC having two radio stations, or programmes, as they were called then. The 'BBC Home Service' and the 'BBC Light Programme'. After the war in 1946 the BBC introduced a third channel and called it 'The Third Programme' (now there's a surprise) which was aimed more at intellectuals rather than us poor working class.

The 'wireless' had two control knobs, one to switch on and off and control volume and the other was the tuner, which you had to turn back and forward to search for the stations.

The accumulators had to be recharged from time to time and there was a bicycle shop, 'Richardsons' I think, just about a hundred yards along from our house in High Street round the corner from the 'Wellwynd'. It was not called 'Wellwynd Street' it was just named 'Wellwynd' but everyone prefixed it with the definite article 'The Wellwynd'.

That's where the recharging could be done. 'Richardsons' had other shops selling radios and other hardware. I would sometimes be asked to carry it there for recharging. I cannot remember how much we paid for that service, probably about 4d or 6d. That's 4pence or 6pence but when writing it down you just used a 'd'.

Pre-decimalisation in 1971 the UK currency was pounds, shillings and pence commonly called L.S.D or written as £.s.d. I believe the letters were abbreviations of roman or latin words but never thought of questioning it then.

Everything today is priced in pounds and pence so an item costing £4.87½ decimal money, (Yes I know, we don't use the half-pence now) would be £4.17shillings and 6pence, written as £4.17.6. using three columns. With decimals of course, we use just two columns.

To further complicate your mind in the old days we also had the half-pence, aye and even farthings, that's a quarter of a penny. I must admit however that although I remember the farthing, the only shop I knew of using a farthing was 'The City Bakeries' in South Bridge Street.

Farthings were sometimes used in pricing their 'tea-bread'. Now, there's another term you may not know of 'tea-bread'. It was the collective name for such items as pancakes, crumpets, tattie scones and sugar topped buns etc.

If my mammy had someone coming in for a cup of tea, she'd send me out to the bakers for some tea-bread. Cakes were only for a special occasion and only the visitor could partake. "Don't dare touch they cakes when Mrs So and So comes in" would be the warning.

My mammy however was renowned for her baking... if she could get the sugar and the butter! Soda scones and apple tarts were her specialty. Because of that I have had life long love of apple pie and I cannot resist a scone with butter and jam! In fact, in the early days of my marriage I used to bake apple tarts myself but I don't think they compared very favourably with my mother's.

Throughout the first 15 years of my life food was rationed, that's why I said 'if she could get the sugar and butter'. That brings me on to the subject of rationing.

RATION BOOKS

I had left school and was working when 'rationing' ended in 1954, although by then most items of food were more plentiful than during the war years and for a about 5 years after the war ended in 1945.

Food rationing began on 8 January 1940, four months after the outbreak of war. I was just over a year old then so obviously I didn't know anything other than 'rations' until I left school. This fact, no doubt, was why I have throughout my life been very frugal, never waste anything or throw out food.

Everyone was issued with ration books by 'The Ministry of Food. Adult ration books were a buff colour and children from 5 to 16 years had blue books. Children under 5 and pregnant women, had green books.

You were required to register with your grocers and butchers to use your ration books with them and they would be supplied with food according to the number of people registered with them. Inside the ration book were pages of coupons to be used when buying various food items. For instance sweets and chocolate etc. were rationed and the pages for these were split into thirteen x 4 week periods numbered from 1 to 13. You had 'E' and 'D' coupons for sweets. I think each 'D' coupon allowed you 2 ounces and 'E' allowed you 4 ounces of sweets. In each 4 week period you would get four D and four E coupons so therefore your total allowance for almost a month would be 24 ounces of sweets. If children nowadays were restricted to that there would be less obesity.

There were no supermarkets in the 1940s and 50s. Shops were specialised and concentrated only on their own categories. There were dairies such as 'Maypole' and 'Buttercup'. These shops only sold milk, cream and cheese, purely dairy products. There were grocery shops such as 'Liptons', 'Galbraiths', and 'Templetons'. Butchers only dealt with meat and poultry, newsagents only sold newspapers, magazines, cigarettes and tobacco. Greengrocers only sold fruit and vegetables and so on.

So you would have a number of shops to go to, to get your 'messages'. Almost everyone however was registered at a 'Co-operative Store'. Each town would have it's own Co-operative Society and Airdrie and Coatbridge was served by the 'Coatbridge Co-operative Society'. I often wondered why there was never one named 'Airdrie Co-operative'.

The supply of grocery items varied each week, some weeks you may be rationed to only 3 eggs per adult and other weeks it would be only one or even none. Other times it would be green books only for eggs, restricted to the under 5's and pregnant mothers.

There's the story I heard that one of the children ran out the house shouting to his mother who was hanging out the washing in the back yard... "Mammy, come quick... my daddy's eating a WHOLE egg"

The number of ration books that you had (the number of persons in the family) would determine how many ounces of butter, sugar, bacon etc. that you were allowed. So when I was sent shopping to the Co-op for the rations I didn't need a shopping list. You just handed over your Co-op membership book and took whatever they gave you. Most times we didn't even pay for it because what you purchased was entered in your book and in the store's book.

You paid your store book weekly. Pay day was a Friday so you got your shopping marked on your book all week but you could ask them to 'draw the line' on the Thursday. This meant that any purchases on a Friday went in to the next weeks account. However, you could not do that on the last week of the 'store quarter'. The 'store quarter' was every three months and your store book had to be paid in full. This gave birth to a couple of sayings... 'The day afore the morra' and the one I heard my mother say so very often... "It's the store quarter and I haven't a curdy"

I also remember queuing at the Co-op offices in High Street Airdrie with my mother to get her 'dividend'. You were a member of the Co-op Society and all the purchases you made in the previous three month period entitled you to a 'dividend' payment, Sometimes that dividend would be about 10% or even 12% of the total payments you made in the three month period so that could be a tidy sum.

Many families counted on that payment to buy school clothing and shoes or special things for Christmas. The 'dividend' was a godsend. This co-operative system continued until the birth of the 'supermarkets' in the early1960s.

Before self-service supermarkets came on the scene all shops had assistants serving the customers behind the counter. Therefore you had to queue to be served, sometimes very long queues.

Much of the produce was not pre-packed so if you wanted 2lbs of sugar the assistant would take a brown paper bag, place it on the scale then ladle in the sugar until the scale read 2lbs.

The bag was then closed with a fold and a twist on the corner and you had your brown paper bag of sugar.

Butter came to the shops in small wooden barrels and for your order of 1lb of butter the assistant would cut a lump of butter then pat it with two wooden pats into a block. From experience they were good at guessing how much to cut off the barrel to start with.

This would have to be weighed on the scale too and a little added or reduced to get the correct weight. This was then wrapped in grease-proof paper. Cheese was usually cut with a wire and weighed and wrapped just like the butter.

Tea came to the shops in very large plywood tea boxes measuring about 3 feet square. These boxes were in great demand to use for storing things and were also commonly used for a 'flitting'.

It was all loose tea as there were no tea bags in the 1940s and early 50s. So tea also had to be individually weighed into paper bags but later it came pre-packed in small paper packets. Our favourite tea was the Co-operative's yellow label 'Ceylon' tea.

Even in the late 1960s when tea bags were common I would still buy loose tea in pre-packed bags because loose tea was less expensive than tea bags, cup for cup... Me being frugal again!

So you can imagine how long it would take to serve a queue of 10 to 15 people having to cut and weigh and wrap all the purchases.

Supermarkets and pre-packing was a boon, it's strange to look back now and believe the system that we operated. As a life long socialist however I regret the demise of the Co-op Society and their dividend system. The Co-operative still exists of course, but as a supermarket and not as a society as before.

My sister, Mary Therese, was 10 years older than me and she had nine children. I spent a lot of my time in her house and after school often went for her 'messages'. I remember on one occasion, she probably only had three children at the time, I went to the Co-op for her rations. The shop assistant said "Oh son, we have tins of John West salmon in, ye better take one for yer mammy". Well she wisnae my mammy, she was my sister but that's besides the point, A tin of salmon was considered a luxury and relatively speaking it was much more expensive than it is today.

I said ok and took the salmon but when my sister saw what price it was, she said she could not afford it, and to think that it cost only half a crown – in today's money that's 12.5 pence. My mother had to buy it from her.

I think I was about 5 years old before I ever saw a banana. Anything that came from overseas was very scarce or mostly not available. The USA however was helping us during the war and they sent us cartons of 'dried eggs'. They came in thick cardboard cartons coated in a waterproof wax to keep it fresh and had an American flag printed on it. It looked like custard powder. You mixed it with water or milk and fried it in the pan. I really loved those dried eggs fried, even more than normal fried eggs.

BERRY PICKING AT BLAIRGOWRIE

I mentioned bananas, which reminds me of when we were picking raspberries in Blairgowrie. I would be only about 8 years old and the first and only 'holiday' I had was to go with my mother and some of my brothers to camp in tents in a field in Blairgowrie and each day go the berry fields to pick raspberries.

This was a means of making some much needed cash for the family, not that I earned much but they couldn't leave an 8 year old at home on his own.

There were some other friends of my mother whose families came too. Each day we would go to the drills of jaggy raspberry bushes and fill 'luggies', wee zinc buckets, then take them to be weighed and paid. I used a small luggie and I think I was paid 3d for each bucket. It took me a long time to fill a bucket and as raspberries are my favourite berry a fair quantity went in to my mouth too.

We travelled to Blairgowrie by train and I still remember leaving from Coatbridge Central station and I think we had one or two changes on the journey. I'm sure one of the junctions was Coupar Angus. Don't know why but that sticks out in my memory.

Our luggage was carried in a smallish wooden chest instead of cases and when we were in the tent this chest was used as a table for eating off, or playing card games.

We slept in large bell-tents and cooking was done in a small hut at the bottom of the field. I didn't do any cooking of course but I looked in and could see numerous women fighting for space at the hobs and all cooking different things and the smell was... well... not too nice, I did not like onions at that time.

Anyway, bananas... That was a fruit that was rarely seen during the war and the austere years thereafter. At the entrance to the field there was a wooden hut where the farmer sold things like bread and rolls and newspapers etc. One day after most people had returned from the fields one of the men thought he'd play a wee prank. He looked up at the hut and noticed there was someone there with a very large cardboard box, so he ran around shouting "There's a man at the hut selling bananas"

So dozens of people ran up to the hut to get bananas before they were sold out. There was no one selling bananas, of course, it was just a hoax. There were however many disappointed, aye and some angry, campers.

In the evenings many of the campers would gather and light a fire and sit around enjoying sing-alongs. There were a few very good singers there. The Old Rugged Cross and Danny Boy were always in the repertoire. We didn't make much money at 'the berries' but the 'holiday' in the country was indeed enjoyable, especially for the young ones.

The Thieving Cat

I said I'd get back to the subject of cats... and dogs.

If you are a cat lover I'm afraid you're not going to like what's coming up so I apologise in advance if you are offended here but I am telling things as I remember them.

Now the 1940s was a very austere period because of the war years and a few years thereafter. Food was rationed there never was any spare cash, everyone was in the same boat, it was make do and mend.

We did have a dog, now and again, probably a stray that found a home with us and we had a few cats over the years. We needed cats to try and keep the mice down but my father didn't have much time for cats, or dogs. We certainly didn't spend any money on them. Cat food and dog food was not a necessity for working class families. Pets ate what scrapings were left or otherwise fended for themselves scavenging outside.

It wasn't uncommon to see dogs sitting outside butcher shops hoping to get a bone or waste scraps. They and cats also scavaged in the brock bins to find scraps of food.

I never heard of anyone taking their cat or dog to a vet, in fact at that time I don't know if there was a vet in Airdrie. If your dog or cat was ill and didn't seem to be recovering and appeared to be suffering you just had them 'put down'.

Airdrie police station in Anderson Street had a large scaled chest which had some kind of gas supply. You would take your dog there and deposit it in the chest (and you got a whiff of the gas in that process) the gas was turned on and the dog got an end to it's suffering.

We were, I'm afraid, less considerate about our feline friends. There were very many stray cats and perhaps because of that and the fact we did not have our pets neutered (that would cost money) cats gave birth to litters of kittens on a regular basis.

Now this is where you cat lovers are going to get a little upset. It was very common and I have to confess that I am guilty here too, to take the new born litter and put them in a hessian bag, maybe an old coal bag, and submerge the bag in a pail of water to drown the poor kittens. Yes, I know, it was cruel and my children and grandchildren scold me for this but, well, it's what happened on a regular occurance in those days.

Our attitude to pets, especially cats, is so much different today. Of course there was no such thing as 'pet insurance' ..huh we didn't even insure ourselves but Nye Bevan was soon to establish our sacred National Health Service, the greatest thing any political party has done in the modern history of politics.

Still on the subject of cats, I said my father did not like them. Well that is an understatement. There was an occasion when my father sat down at the kitchen table to eat his meal, a fish dish. He got up to do something and the cat we had at that time took this opportunity to jump up onto the table and start eating the fish.

To say that pater was angry is an understatement.

Now the old gas cooker we had in the scullery was fairly small compared with todays models and it did not have a closed and sealed oven compartment. This oven had legs about 5 inches high and the bottom of the oven was completely open.

My father made up his mind that the poor cat had just commited her final crime and was sentenced to death by gassing. He eventually managed to catch the cat and he bundled it into the oven, closed the door and turned on the gas but didn't light it.

He thought it would only take a minute or two for the cat to die of gas poisoning. He forgot however that the oven base was open and so the cat naturally escaped underneath. He was concerning himself with turning on the correct gas knob that he didn't even see the cat scurrying out the scullery.

The daft eejit could have blown us all to smithereens. The cat used one of it's nine lives and lived another day... to steal another meal.

MY FATHER

My father was not born in this century (the 21st), he was not born during the last century, he was actually born in the century before that. When I say that to people their reaction is one of disbelief, so much so that they are prepared to wager a bet on it and that has happened on one or two occasions.

Queen Victoria was on the throne when he made it into the 19th century by a few months, he was born in 1898.

I suppose, deep down I did like my father, simply because he was my father and perhaps I was duty bound to do so, but I certainly did not admire him. I could not see that there was really anything admirable about him and I cannot recall any occasion, when I was a child, we did even one thing together, as fathers and sons should be doing and do much more today.

He never taught me to ride a bike, fly a kite, read a book, go a walk, or play any games other than card games. He did however give me a cigarette on occasions when I was still at primary school, what the hell was he thinking about?

There was really no father/son relationship as such and I'm sure it was the same with all my siblings.

Times were different then and I suppose it was not uncommon for many fathers to neglect their fatherly duties or perhaps they thought bringing up the children was a job solely for the mother.

The real reason of course, for his parental neglect, was his addiction to drink. A very common fault in the working classes in the early part of the 20th century and to a degree it is still the same today.

It certainly never occurred to me that I should feel deprived because of this lack of involvement with my father and I never did. Nor did it affect me in thinking that there was something missing in life. I just accepted that I had very little connection with my father, I suppose you don't miss what you have not experienced.

I was very well aware however that my father was a very heavy drinker. He would be off to work in his cobbler shop before I got up in the morning to go to school and he never came home early.

The pubs in Airdrie closed at 9pm so he seldom appeared home until after closing time. Invariably I was in bed before he got home so really I saw very little of my father in my first eleven years of life.

Occasionally, when we were playing some street games in the summer evenings such as 'hide and seek' or 'one after all', I would meet him in High Street and I would like that because he would dip into his waistcoat pocket and give me a three-penny bit. That would let me go to 'Ben Bianci's' chip shop at the top of South Bridge Street and get two-pence worth of chips… my favourite food… and still have a penny left!

I also recall occasions when he was drunk and shouting and swearing at my mother. It really frightened me when he would grab the table cover and send everything on the kitchen table flying. Witnessing such actions, it is not surprising that I didn't feel deprived of such fatherly care or company.

I cannot say that he hit me at any time, well I seen very little of him in any case, but I remember one occasion when I would only have been about four or five years old, he lifted me and held my bare feet under the water tap. It was freezing cold water, there was no hot water in the house. I was terrified and it was painfully cold. I don't know why this episode stands out in my mind but it must have had a frightening affect on me at the time.

Contrary to some train of thought, however, that children experiencing neglect or abuse or cruelty by their father can result in similar behaviour when they are adults, I was adamant that if ever I got married and had children I would certainly not try to emulate him. I had two sisters and three brothers and I'm sure all of them thought as I did on this matter.

My three brothers, two sisters and myself, for many years, smoked cigarettes. Eventually we realised the dangers and stupidity of smoking and all of us dropped the habit.

It is also interesting to note that while my three brothers and I, throughout our life, could all enjoy alcohol, and on occasion a little too much I'll admit, none of us let alcohol in any way control our life or result in neglect of the family as it did our father.

Thankfully his example gave all of us the determination to be dutiful fathers and I'm sure if you were to ask any of the 36 grandchildren which our mother had, they would verify this fact.

It could, of course, have worked the other way and his love of alcohol could have influenced and encouraged us to go down that road. Thankfully we all had a bit more common sense.

In later years, however, I got to thinking about a quote I read which went something like 'Don't condemn or criticise a person ... because you have not walked in their shoes'.

My father as a young man, little more than a boy, about 18 years of age was caught up in the First World War. He, in fact, was engaged in possibly one of the worst battles of this horrendous conflict... 'Passchendaele'. He was wounded by bullet or shrapnel and eventually shipped home to military hospital in Lymm in Cheshire.

This experience as a young teenager might well have had a tremendous impact on his life and I never gave this any thought until very recently. In fact, although I knew he was injured in World War I, I was actually in my seventies before my brother Joe enlightened me that he was actually wounded at Passchendaele. So, in retrospect, perhaps I should judge my father much more charitably.

He was however, the reason we - the family that is - moved to

Calderbank, minus my father.

He went to work at his cobbler shop in Sunnyside Road Coatbridge one day and when he returned to our house in High St Airdrie that evening we had all moved out, taking with us what little furniture and possessions we had.

I was just around 10 or 11 years old at the time, so it would be in 1949/50. The set of circumstances surrounding his drinking and the deteriorating relationship with my mother and the rest of the family required a solution.

Accrued debts incurred as a result of his alcohol abuse, would have resulted in what meagre possessions we had in our rented home being 'pinned'.

That was the word I heard then but later realised that the correct word is poinded, a Scotish law permitting a Sheriff court to poind the goods of a debtor to pay a debt.

My mother saw a way out; our cousin, Hugh McGoldrick, had recently taken occupation of shop premises in Calderbank and began operating it as a cobbler shop. Along with the shop came an upstairs 4 bedroom flat. This was to be my mother's answer to her many prayers.

This flat was available to rent and as a family we were very close to Hugh, or 'Sonny' as he was more often called due to his father also being named Hugh, our Uncle Hughie.

He too was a cobbler. That trade seemed to run in our family, my father and his brother Joe were cobblers.

Anyway, I was too young to understand the plan my mother and older brothers hatched with our cousin for us to move in to the available flat. I do however clearly remember the 'flittin'.

In our large front bedroom in Airdrie we had a massive mahogany wardrobe with a huge wide drawer at the bottom. This wardrobe probably measured about five feet wide and more than six feet in height.

The entry door to the flat we were moving to in Calderbank was situated midway down the 'close' and the inside staircase took a semi circular right turn halfway up. The wardrobe therefore was a big problem despite removing the large drawer.

The upshot was that it got stuck on the bend, it was manoeuvred and nudged one way then another and eventually became immovable. Impatience and frustration took over and more force was used resulting in the wood splitting in various places. More force and more splitting and eventually it was dismantled using hammers. Dismantled is probably the wrong word, as all we had in the end was firewood.

THE COUPON'S UP!

My father continued to live at the house in High Street Airdrie and after a short period my brother Jim, who was four years older than me and the second youngest in the family, began to go back occasionally to visit him. Partly through pity and partly because we thought it was perhaps a duty or at least the charitable thing to do.

It would be Saturdays usually and we would play cards along with him and a boy we were friendly with when we lived there, Willie Jack. My father bet on the football pools every week so a ritual on these Saturday nights was to check to see if he had a winning line of 7 draws or 8 draws, depending on which Football Pools Company you bet with.

One could bet on the 'treble chance'; selecting 8 games resulting in a draw or on the 'penny points'; a selection of fixtures of which you had to predict a home win, an away win or a draw.

The treble chance bet was the one that offered the jackpot prizes and therefore it was the most popular and the one that my father used.

There was no Lottery operating then, the football pools was its equivalent. Everyone dreamed of winning the pools.

The biggest pools companies were Littlewoods and Vernons but there were other smaller companies, I can only remember two names; ITP and Shermans. It was one of these two pools companies that my father bet with. I think he did so because theirs was a 7selection line as opposed to 8 draws with Littlewoods and Vernons.

The maximum amount you could win in those days was £75,000, an absolute fortune! The cost of a new built 3 bedroom bungalow at that time would be under £2,000, so a win of that size could buy you 37 homes! How much is that worth in today's money?

The amount paid out depended, of course, on how many draws there were on the coupon that week.

If there were only 7, 8 or 9 draws you were assured of a good or a possible maximum 'jackpot' prize.

If there were 12 or more draws then the payout would be very much smaller. The pools companies, after they deducted their profits, would share the remaining 'pool' of money with the prize-winners. I suppose that was why they were called 'pools'.

There were less regulations governing the pools companies in the 1940s and some weeks during winter when a number of games would be called off due to snow or other weather conditions, the company could declare the pools 'void' and presumably your amount staked would be carried over to the next week.

On the occasions when a number of games were called off, one Pool company may pay out on the 'penny points' but declare the 'treble chance' void and another company vice versa, although mostly they seemed to come to the same decisions.

My father had a system for the treble chance based on the number 7 so he must have bet on a coupon that required you to select 7 fixtures from a total of around 52.

His first line selected the numbers 1,7,14,21,28,35 and 42. The next line would start 49, but there would only be 3 numbers up to the total 52 so he would start at the beginning again and miss any number already used in the first line. So the second line read 49, 2, 10, 18, 26, 34 and 43. He continued in this system until all the numbers to 52 were used, that would give him seven lines before all the numbers were exhausted and he would start a new set of lines beginning with the number 2. His first line then would be 2, 9, 16, 23, 30, 37, 44. He continued in this fashion until all the available columns on the coupon were completed.

"This system means that I must have each and every draw somewhere on my coupon", he would assuredly point out.

"Aye Daddy, but the secret is, to get seven of them in one line".

The coupon was in a graph form with the fixtures listed on the left hand side and the remainder of space divided into columns, probably about 20 columns in total so if you used them all, as my father did, you would be betting 20 lines and I think the stake was 3 pence per line.

He kept neatly written cards with these 20 lines of numbers and I think it was Thursdays when the coupons had to be completed and posted to the company in pre-printed envelopes enclosing a postal order to the value of your total stakes.

He used carbon paper between 2 copies of the coupon to ensure he was getting an accurate copy and the whole exercise would probably take him an hour or two to complete.

The checking of the results on a Saturday night was an even longer operation. The only way to get the football results was from the evening newspapers so he would buy The Evening Times, The Evening News and the Evening Citizen.

There were early and late editions of these papers and sometimes some results were not included in the list of results on the front page and one had to check the 'late results' column on the back page to find the missing scores.

So, most Saturday nights, my brother Jim, our pal Willie Jack and I would each have a copy of a newspaper and my father would check each line shouting out the team names and we would scan the paper for the result and relate it to him.

Week after week there was never a line with seven draws… until one Saturday, it could have been in the 1947/48 winter as that was a very severe and snowy winter. Many games were not played because of the weather and this particular week there was only seven draws on the coupon!

I vividly remember how my father got really excited and frustrated! On one particular line he went through the fixtures… one draw… two draws… three draws… four draws. "Jesus Christ", he said. I don't think he at that moment was appealing for divine intervention, or maybe he was.

He was getting impatient on us finding the relevant scores. Five draws… "Oh my God".

"Plymouth Argyle".

"It's a draw too daddy 2-2".

"Jesus Christ, that's six draws! Reading versus Portsmouth".

The *Reading* v *Portsmouth* fixture was listed as late score! Each of us, highly excited at this point, was scanning the newspapers but couldn't find the score so we started looking for the 'late results'.

Frustration and desperation overcame my father and he grabbed one of the papers from Jim's hand.

"Gimme the fuckin paper for Christ sake!"

Eventually the score was found in the late news.

Another draw 2-2 … that made it 7 draws… THE COUPON WAS UP!

"THE COUPON IS UP!!! IT'S UP!!!"

"Jesus Christ", "Jesus Christ".

There was little else he seemed capable of saying and he didn't say much more for a while. He was deep in concentration.

Soon after the realisation of winning the pools began to penetrate, his next thought must have been whisky!

He went down to Alex Reid's pub just a few doors along High Street or maybe it was Mulveys at the top of Bell Street. I think he talked them in to giving him a couple of bottles of whisky 'on tick'.

The Sunday newspapers didn't carry the payout details of how much you won if you had 7 draws, how much for 6 draws etc., that was normally printed in the Monday editions. They did however indicate usually if any of the pools companies declared any sections void.

The Sunday Post and Sunday Mail were purchased and revealed that Littlewoods and Vernons declared the 'Penny Points' void because of the number of fixtures cancelled, but they would pay out on the 'Treble Chance'.

That was good news for my father and there was no indication that the Pool he used, let's say it was Shermans, had declared any voids so as far as he was concerned the treble chance was 'on'.

The Daily Record on Monday however confirmed that Littlewoods and Vernons would pay out on the 'Treble Chance' and the 'Penny

Points' were void but Shermans and ITP Pools would pay out on the 'Penny Points' but declared the 'Treble Chance' VOID!!!!

"It's a bloody misprint, that can't be right. Get me an Express"

We bought the Daily Express, Daily Mail, Daily Mirror, even another copy of the Daily Record in case they corrected their earlier 'mistake'. All of them confirmed the treble chance was void. He won nothing! - absolutely nothing!

I have often thought of how our lives would have changed had he bet with Littlewoods or Vernons pools that week. Many times I also wondered what thoughts must have gone through his mind.

It would have turned many men to drink as the saying goes, but then he was already down that road!

It would appear that my father was not destined to win anything on the football pools. There was another occasion, a few years later, when he had a number of draws on one line.

This time it was less than the maximum draws, perhaps just 4 or 5 draws but he would still partake in the pool of prizes.

This particular week he should have won around £28. Not a lot of money, but for some working people it would equate to more than three week's wages at that time.

I was still at school at St Patricks Coatbridge, it must have been around 1951/52 and after school I would go most days to my father's cobbler shop in Sunnyside Road, Coatbridge.

I would help strip soles and heels, go to the leather merchants shop for supplies, take shoes to the stitcher's shop to have soles stitched to the uppers or deliver repairs to the customer's homes.

One day he asked me to go to the post office on my way home, buy a postal order for the amount of his stake on the football pool and make it payable to Vernons. After his experience with Shermans he deserted them and started with a more reliable Pool company!

He didn't have any of Vernon's own pre-printed envelopes at his work so he said to me,

"Buy a stamped addressed envelope from the post office. Put this coupon and the postal order you get, into the envelope, seal it and post

it. Make sure it goes before the post office shuts or it will be too late"
Well, I followed his instructions to the letter!
I bought the postal order and a stamped addressed envelope. I made
the postal order payable to Vernons. I put the football coupon and the
postal order in the envelope, sealed it and put it in the post box.
This was the occasion when he would have won around £28 but the
envelope was 'returned to sender' by the Post Office because there
was no address written on the front of the envelope!
So again, he received no winnings!
He was very angry with me and I was in tears.
"Never mind your crocodile tears", I distinctly remember his words.
He called me all the stupid so and so eejits you can imagine, using a
few, foul mouthed adjectives.
I tried to justify my action of posting an envelope without an address.
"You told me to get a stamped-addressed envelope... if it was an
addressed envelope, I don't need to address it, you didn't say to write
an address on it".
That didn't hold any water with him. I just avoided him for a while.
I got to thinking, the problem resulted from the commonly used
term 'stamped-addressed envelope', when really it should just be a
'stamped envelope'. That was my defence, I took everything literally,
but truly I was a stupid eejit that time!
Having a regular bet on the football pools didn't qualify my father as
a gambler but he did also like an occasional punt on the horses. There
was no National Lottery then and if there were he would no doubt
have entered that regularly.
In the 1950s gambling was illegal, there were no casinos, they were
only for the rich and famous in Monte Carlo.
At racecourses, just as it is today, there were bookmakers and I presume
that was the only gambling that was permitted legally. Even playing
Bingo was illegal and police would occasionally raid premises where
it was being played and participants would be charged with illegal
gambling.
One of these establishments in Airdrie was the Labour Party club,
'The Shack' as it was called, a very large wooden hut down the 'Pit

Close' off High Street just a stone's throw from our house.

I remember one evening my father was playing bingo (I think at that time it was called 'Housey Housey') in the shack when the police arrived in their 'black-marias'. They conveyed all the 'gamblers' to the police station in Anderson Street.

He was in the same police van as local worthy, wee Harry Roy who was even smaller than my father. Both of them had a great sense of humour and apparently kept everyone amused in the van while waiting for the prosecutions to be processed.

Although gambling was breaking the law, there were however lots of illegal 'bookies' in every town and village.

I was told that before he was married my father 'ran a book' with 'runners' in all the iron works in Coatbridge. These runners would collect the betting slips and money and take it to my father and I presume they would also take back any winnings to the lucky punters. I was also told that my father was the first 'bookie' in the Monklands area to pay out winnings on the same day as the race was won. 'Shovel betting' it was called. I cannot fathom out why it was so called.

Apparently, numerous police raids on his mother's home where he would try to flush down the toilet the incriminating betting slips, eventually persuaded him to give up his spell as a bookie.

Sometimes I had to go to the bookies with his 'line', a piece of paper, with the bet indicated thereon and at the bottom would be his nom de plume. Every punter used their nom de plume on the line and the bookie would know who the punter was. My father's nom de plume was 'x me x'. I asked him the meaning of this and he said, "Kiss me Arse".

I followed his example of an odd bet on the horses and I would always use his nom de plume. Even when I was still at school I would sometimes put three-pence each way on a horse and give it to a bookie who operated through a close half way up Jackson Street Coatbridge, round the corner from my school.

Through a close was a popular place for illegal bookies to be situated. I remember the one who sat on the toilet seat of an outside toilet at the top of High Street and Davidson Street just across the road from

Mulvey's pub.

He was an obese man, locally referred to as 'Big Rab'. He gave meaning to a term we commonly used when you saw someone wearing an item of clothing that was far too big for them; "God, that jacket you're wearing would fit Big Rab".

That was a terrible insult to inflict on anyone and even to this day when I'm trying on clothes in a shop and the item is too big I still say, "That would fit Big Rab".

A BIG WIN ON THE HORSES

Apart from his 'system' for the Football Pools, my father had a system for betting horses. In gambling, he thought you must have a system! "In a small race of less than eight runners, always bet on the third favourite", he would say. When there was a big field of 15 or more runners … "bet the seventh in the betting".

I cannot remember him having any big winnings on the horses or at least he didn't make us aware of any.

There was only one occasion when I had a really good win on the horses and it was shared with my brother Joe.

It was October 1962 and I remember it because it was the day before our 88year old Grandmother died. She lived with my mother for the last few years of her life.

My brother Joe and I were railway booking clerks and both of us were on an early shift that day.

After work Joe came over to visit our Granny, we called her Maw, and after a wee while Joe and I got around to looking at the racing section of the newspapers.

We lived in an upstairs five-apartment council flat in Fir View, Calderbank and the local bookie, John Freel, lived in the flat below with his wife and 8 or 9 children.

His betting shop was in an old property adjacent to our house. Betting shops only became legal the previous year 1961 and they were springing up everywhere.

Prior to legalisation the police would occasionally raid them and the bookie would pay any fines the punters incurred.

We studied form in the newspaper that day and each of us selected a number of horses. We settled on a selection of five horses and decided to bet ten sixpenny doubles. Ten doubles at sixpence each, amounted to five shillings, that would be two shillings and sixpence each, half a crown.

"Will we treble them?".

Five horses gives you ten trebles.

"That would be another two and sixpence each".

"Ach naw, if we get one double up we'll be lucky".

"Aye yer right I suppose, OK".

We went down to the bottom pub and had a pint and while there we discovered our first two selections had won. "We've got a double up".

We then made our way up to the betting shop and waited for the next race.

Another winner! "God that's three doubles and still two more races to come".

We were getting excited by then. The last two horses were in races at the same time at two different racecourses… Both of them won, that meant we had ten doubles.

The incredible thing however was the starting prices of these winners. The five starting prices were: 100/8, 100/8, 100/9, 6/1 and 4/1.

Everyone in the betting shop knew of our great luck and one man, Con Murray, who was our brother Jim's father-in-law, was congratulating us.

"Con, I feel we can't do any wrong today, bet …", and I mentioned another horse that I had selected but it didn't get into our final five.

"Oh, you're too late, that has just won at 4/1".

It was that kind of day, probably something you'll do only once in a lifetime.

For our five-shilling stake we got £35.5 shillings to share. It may not sound much now but that was about 4 or 5 weeks wages for me.

Had we invested another half crown each and bet the ten trebles we would have won an additional £330, a massive amount.

Our Maw (grandmother), died the next day and the following evening at the wake when the house was packed with mourners saying the rosary, the bookie was kneeling beside me in the lobby.

"Any of the regulars in my betting shop would have trebled them", said John.

"Aye" I replied, "We would have been collecting over £300".

"Do ye think so?" he said!

One way (perhaps the only one), in which my father did have an impression on me was his sense of humour and I have inherited a bit of that, hopefully the good parts, but to be honest I think the family are a bit bored with my attempts at humour – 'Oh God, another 'Daddy' joke.

He always tried to make light of everything and no matter who he was talking to, or what the subject of conversation was, he'd try to butt in with funny remarks.

Sometimes they were funny, sometimes satirical, sometimes downright cruel and insensitive. He didn't mind offending people but he got away with it because mostly his audience would see the funny side. Being only about 5 foot 4 inches in height and never to my knowledge been known to be in any physical scraps, I would have thought that he must have taken a few risks in the pubs if he sarcastically offended one of his fellow drinkers. Maybe his height saved him... or maybe he was paying for the drinks.

An example of how blunt he could be and still try to introduce humour to the situation is evident in this incident.

It was after my father re-joined the family and moved into our house in Fir View, Calderbank, it would be around 1952 or 1953.

My mother was a member of the Women's Guild at the church. So also was another lovely woman, in the interests of anonymity, let's call her Mrs Connolly. With a son a priest and a daughter a nun Mrs Connolly was a devout Catholic woman, a devout Catholic family indeed.

My father was at the bus stop one day and he and Mrs Connolly got involved in discussion, which it appears developed into a kind of disagreement on some subject. Knowing my father and the language he would use when he felt the argument or discussion was not going in his favour, it appears that he told Mrs Connolly to "Go and have a shite".

She was obviously, and justifiably, offended at his language, so much so that she did mention it to my mother when at the 'Women's Guild' meeting, although she did not relate verbatim the exchange of words. My mother did confront my father on the matter and said to him, "Mrs Connolly was really upset at whatever you said to her at the bus stop, what on earth did you say to the woman?"

My daddy didn't enlighten her but said he'd apologise next time he met her.

A short time later he told us that he sorted out the problem with Mrs Connolly, he said that he again met her at the bus stop and said to her "Mrs Connolly, remember the last time we spoke I told you to 'go and have a shite', ... well don't bother your arse!"

Somehow, I don't think she would have seen or appreciated the humorous connection!

THE COBBLER SHOPS

In my memory, my daddy only operated from one cobbler shop, in Sunnyside Road Coatbridge but before that he had a shop in Clark Street Airdrie, which his brother Joe ran for him. I was told that he had other shops, there was one in High Street Airdrie. In the photo section of this book you can see my father pictured with two others outside his High Street shop. You may notice that the embossed lettering on the window reads *'GRANT BOOTMAKER REPAIRS - NEATLY AND CHEAPTLY DONE'*.

Please note the spelling of the word 'cheaply' on the window, it is spelt 'cheaptly'. Maybe that is a very old spelling of the word but I think it was just how the Irish would say cheaply putting a 'T' there.

I remember being told that he had five cobbler shops but I would doubt that he operated them all at the one time. He did have at least two going at the same time as is evident from a promotional advert printed on card backed with blotting paper.

There were no ball point pens in those days so blotting paper was used extensively when writing with pen and ink.

Apparently, he had been earning lots of money in those days but his drinking and supplying drink to his friends soon squandered the money. When you are buying drinks for everyone you are sure to have lots of friends so by the time I came along in 1938, money was in short supply.

There were many stories of things that went on in his shops.

It was a trade that, for some reason, seemed to attract handicapped people. There was one worker with a wooden leg, (am I allowed to say that now or should I say prosthetic leg?) he was called 'the pin' and two brothers, Matt and Pat Costello who were deaf and dumb.

Another incident to illustrate my Daddy's satirical sense of humour was the occasion that one morning on opening the shop they caught and killed a mouse.

When it came to the break for lunch everyone would settle down and open their 'piece'; sandwiches wrapped in paper.

Most of those working in the shop would have been Catholic and at that time those of that faith didn't eat meat on Fridays, so it would normally be cheese that would be on their 'pieces'.

Unknown to the Costellos, my daddy had opened Matt's sandwich wrapping and took the cheese off the bread and replaced it with the dead mouse.

Just as Matt raised the bread to his mouth my daddy stopped him and said,

"It's Friday Matt, ye can't eat meat the day".

Matt shooed him away, and though he could not speak he certainly could make loud sounds saying... "eeeze!...eeeze!" and then he attempted again to eat the bread. He was stopped once more... "Friday... No meat!"

Matt was getting angry by this time and decided to show everyone that it was cheese on his sandwich and opened the bread!

When he saw the mouse where the cheese should have been all hell broke loose. What Matt lacked in speaking ability he more than made up for in loud roars and gesticulations, he clearly indicated his displeasure at the prank.

Despite Matt's angry reaction, had the opportunity to engage in a similar prank arisen the next day, my father would not have let the opportunity slip.

A couple of doors down from his shop in Sunnyside Road there was an ice cream café, run by an Italian who spoke broken English.

All the ice cream shops in Airdrie and Coatbridge, and I imagine throughout the West of Scotland, were run by first second or third generation Italians and so their cafes and fish and chip shops were called 'The Tallies'. This was not in any way a derogatory term, it was just an abbreviation of Italian and the Tallies did not take offence at it, as far as I knew.

People from Newcastle were called Geordies, Welsh were Taffies, Australians were Aussies and nobody felt insulted with the use of these terms, so it puzzled me why in later years, that Pakistanis should so strongly object to the abbreviation 'Paki'. So why is it, that only that abbreviation, is considered so politically incorrect? In any case, I do not and did not use that term.

We called black people 'darkies' or 'coloured' and again we did not consider that to be in any way offensive. They were dark skinned and that was a reasonable description. We even called many of our pet dogs that were black or black and white, 'Darkie', it was certainly not meant in any way as an insult. When it was pointed out that they preferred the term blacks then we have used that term since then.

As a young boy in the 40s and early 50s, it was very rarely that we saw any black or coloured people in the Monklands area and if you did they would be stared at simply because it was so unusual and they were dressed differently. That was just a natural curious reaction.

One of the few places we would encounter foreigners was in the area around a model lodging house, situated just off Jackson Street in Coatbridge. The lodgers were mainly Asians or Orientals working on the ships in Glasgow and of course they would be wearing traditional clothing, which was quite intriguing to us.

This building used as a lodging house, later became a knitwear factory and in fact my first job after leaving school was in this very place, 'Queenesta Knitwear'.

It took two buses from Calderbank to Coatbridge to get to Queenesta Knitwear.

I started at 8am and worked until 6pm Monday to Friday with a one hour break at lunchtime. I was paid £1.19s 7p clear. The top line was £2.3shillings but there was 3 shillings and 5 pence deducted for national insurance. So, my hourly rate for a 45hour week was just over 7pence an hour, and that is in old money when there was 240 pennies to the pound. Slave labour. I was only 15 years old at that time.

I was only employed there for about three months until I started with British Railways as a booking clerk.

My occupation in the knitwear factory was a 'draw-threader'. The cuffs of cardigans and pullovers were knitted on the machines in long strips and separated by threads. My duty was to snip the threads at one side, then pull the thread through thereby separating each cuff, I would then put them into bundles of 24.

It was boring. Other workers had similarly boring tasks so it was not surprising that at any opportunity, when the foreman was out of sight, some of us would have a little fun and start throwing things at one another.

Unfortunately, one of the rags thrown landed on one of the machines and broke lots of needles and stopped production. The foreman was back on the scene immediately, having heard a reduction in sound as one of the machines was incapacitated. He went berserk. A couple of hours production time was lost and there were a few guilty looking faces, but no one accepted responsibility.

It was a long working day, so we had a short ten-minute tea break in the morning and afternoon plus of course the 1hour lunch break (which was not paid for).

Like most other employees, I carried 'my piece' to work each day. This consisted of a few sandwiches, bread and cheese or bread and jam usually.

One day for a change, I had bread and syrup. I put my sandwiches wrapped in paper on the radiator behind the table I was working at. At the first tea break I opened the wrapping and took out a sandwich. The hot radiator had almost cooked the syrup into a hard candy and the bread was solid like cardboard. It didn't stop me from eating it though, I couldn't afford to buy anything from the tea trolley that did the rounds in the factory.

Very near the 'Queenesta Knitwear' around the corner on Jackson Street, the Co-operative Society used horse drawn vehicles for much of their deliveries and street trading, even into the 1950s. They had very swish looking bakery vans which looked like a caravan, the horse reins went through the front window and the driver was always covered, the customers stepped inside the van to be served. I suppose that was necessary to combat the Scottish weather.

Milk wagons were open as were the coal wagons and they were just flat, no sides or roofs. It did not matter if it rained as there was no need for protection from inclement weather. Horse feed bags were often hung around their necks, the drivers would stop for a break and take a smoke while the horse enjoyed its feed. What goes in must also come out so the streets were littered with horse shit, but it was often lifted by those growing vegetables in their gardens so normally it wouldn't lie in the street for very long. We never spent money on garden fertilisers then. Half way up Jackson Street in Coatbridge was where the horse stables and depot for the Co-operative wagons were situated, as I walked past there each morning going to school I got a real strong healthy smell of horseshit, but I have never found that odour to be too displeasing, unlike dog deposits.

Sunnyside Road Cobbler Shop, Coatbridge

My oldest brother, John, was a time served fitter having been apprenticed to his trade in Pickering's engineering works in Wishaw. He wore a boiler suit to his work and he had a spare one, which my daddy thought he could wear to his work.

He would normally always wear a waistcoat both at his work or when he was dressed. Although he had a protective leather bib to be strapped over his waistcoat, he often did not put it on.

The constant trimming of the leather soles and heels as he held the shoe with one hand and had the shoe pressed against his chest, the very sharp 'James Otley' knife would occasionally cut and tear his waistcoats.

That was the most common item of apparel he would buy. He was always on the lookout for spare waistcoats. My Daddy never rolled up his sleeves when he was working and he never wore a belt, he only wore braces to keep his trousers up. Boiler suits from the engineering works probably only came in one size and one had to wear a belt to get a good fit.Being about five inches smaller than John, this boiler suit was way far too long in the legs for my daddy. He wouldn't wear a belt to adjust the length; his answer was simply to cut about ten inches off the legs. It was now about the right length, but the crutch of the trousers was actually down near his knees. It didn't seem to bother him and perhaps he didn't know how stupid he looked.

Anyway, he decided after a couple of days to discard the boiler suit. He related to us the reason,

"I was walking past the ice cream shop and the Tally was standing outside, after I passed he shouted after me".

He then attempted to copy the Italian's broken English,

"Hey, Mr Cobbler, you got no arse?… your arse trail on ground".

That was an excellent description, so it eventually got through to him that the boiler suit was not for him, it was making him a laughing stock.

I was the youngest son and my brothers John and Joe both had spells of working in the cobbler shop in Sunnyside Road, Coatbridge.

When I attended School in Coatbridge it was then my turn and I would go there most days after school. By this time in his life, alcohol had full control over him and when someone came in with a repair, 9 shillings for new soles and 12 shillings and sixpence for soles and heels, he would suggest to them that; "If you pay for it now I'll get it delivered to your house tomorrow afternoon, when my boy comes out of school".

Invariably they would agree. He would then put on his jacket, get the already written notice on a piece of cardboard 'Back in 5 Minutes' and pin it on the door. He would be off to a pub for a beer and a whisky, maybe more than one, and be back again usually in about 15 or 20 minutes.

On the occasions when I was in the shop, he dispensed with the need for the notice on the door. Sometimes I would arrive at the shop after school, see the notice and have to await his arrival. The strange thing was, although he always seemed to smell of alcohol, he never appeared to be unsteady on his feet and never swayed or slurred, as you would expect. He had two bad legs, one shorter than the other as a result of his wound in one leg from World War I and a broken femur in his other leg.

The broken femur apparently occurred when the rope holding a number of bales of leather, (i.e.- the hide of a full cow), snapped and fell on his upper leg, breaking the femur.

With two legs of different lengths the resultant limp perhaps concealed or fudged any unsteadiness caused by the alcohol consumption.

I would get the job of delivering repairs and in some cases collect the money due, if they had not been prepaid.

Sometimes the delivery was in nearby homes and sometimes it would be in Gartsherrie, Townhead or even in Glenboig.

"What about ma bus fare?", I would ask.

"Take the money out of what they pay you".

That was OK if I had money of my own but most often my pockets were empty, so I had to walk on the outward journey at least!

There was a period when I had the use of a bicycle, which some customer had left in the shop to be collected at a later date.

It was in the shop for a week or so and my Daddy told me to use it to do the deliveries. That seemed OK with me and in fact I started to go to school using this bike, as I did not posses a bike at home.

This situation continued for several weeks. One day he asked me to make a delivery to a house in Townhead, which I duly did, on the bike!

On returning to the shop my Daddy said, "Did she say anything about the bike?"

"No, why should she?"

"Well it's her son's bike. It was her who left it here".

He hadn't the decency to tell me beforehand, but on second thoughts, if he had, I would have been too embarrassed to go to her house. The woman's son came for the bike shortly after that. I think he had started to attend a seminary for the priesthood and this was him home, for a short spell.

Fortunately, the bike was in the shop when he came and I never heard anything further on the matter, but I did miss that bike!

In the 1950s, trading hours for shops and even department stores were roughly 9am to 6pm, Mondays to Saturdays, and they closed for about one hour or even one and a half hours at lunchtime. All shops were closed on a Sunday. Most railway services were closed on Sundays and bus and tram services were limited.

On one day midweek, it would be the merchants half day, which meant that all the shops in the town would be closed for the day at 1pm.

Each town would have a weekly 'half day' and in Airdrie and Coatbridge that day was a Wednesday. In Glasgow, it was a Tuesday. My father however rarely closed his shop and I know he would not have been a member of any trader's association.

Apart from Christmas Day and possibly New Years Day I think he only closed on two other days a year, Glasgow Fair Monday and the Wednesday of that week.

It is interesting to note too that many shops in the town would close for annual holidays for the whole two weeks of the Glasgow Fair.

He did not close for the half day on a Wednesday each week, though occasionally he might finish a little earlier than normal because business would be a lot lighter when all the other shops were closed. This situation gave rise to a very funny incident, but not so funny for the owner of a lovely wall clock.

I was in the shop early one Wednesday afternoon when someone came in with a glass cased wall clock measuring about 2ft high x 1ft wide and 6 or 7 inches deep. It had a brass disc pendulum and indeed was a very attractive wall clock.

"The watchmakers shop a few doors down is closed this afternoon" said the man with the clock.

"Do you think I could leave it here and you could give it to him in the morning?"

"I don't want to have to carry it all the way home again".

"Aye sure, I'll do that for ye".

"It's just stopped going, I think maybe I have overwound it, tell the watchmaker I'll call in tomorrow".

The man was quite relieved that he didn't have to cart the heavy clock back home and departed quite happily.

That Wednesday was very quiet, no work left to be done and my Daddy stood looking at the clock for a while. It was similar in style to the one we, and thousands of others, had in their living rooms at home but this one looked a lot more stylish than ours.

Purely out of boredom having nothing to occupy his time (it would not have entered my father's mind that the shop could have benefitted from a good tidy up and cleaning) he decided that he would have a look at the clock… "it's probably just been overwound".

He proceeded to open the wooden framed glass door and start to investigate the various moving parts of the clock. He didn't know what he was doing but he tried to do something with the large coiled spring. Suddenly, and making a great noise, the spring sprung loose and expanded to many times it size, simultaneously knocking loose many other parts of the clock's mechanism.

"Oh Jesus Christ, …whit do ah do now".

He was obviously concerned and knew there was nothing he could do to put it back to the condition he received it in. He gathered the parts that went airborne and returned them to join all the other parts inside the clock.

It took almost half an hour to get the spring and everything else back in and still be able to close the glass door.

After a lot of thought was given to the problem he told me of his decision. He would take it to the watchmaker, I think he was Polish, explain that a man had left the clock with us to pass it on to him today.

"We left it on the counter and I had no more mind of it as I was working through the back".

He sounded convincing.

"Then there was this loud smash noise, Christ it gave me a helluva fright", sounding even more convincing.

"Ah came through the front and there it was, just as you see it now Whit a bloody fright I got!"

Somehow, I don't think the watchmaker believed his story and I understand he was a bit reluctant to take the clock, but eventually he did.

I never did hear the outcome or if the owner ever approached my father. He just never told us.

CALDERBANK

As I said earlier, the reason our family moved to Calderbank, just two miles from Airdrie, was to get away from our father. This meant that at ten or eleven years of age I was moved to a new area and thereby left all the friends and pals I knew.

I still attended the same primary school, St Margaret's in Hallcraig Street Airdrie, and so still had my school friends during school hours.

I think there was only one other Calderbank boy who attended St Margaret's at that time and his surname was also Grant, Arthur Grant. Probably due to this, we became very close friends, a strong friendship through boyhood and teenage years and in fact lasted a lifetime. About fourteen years later, Arthur and I married two of the six Fagan sisters from Newarthill but that's another story later in the book.

Arthur was also a recent 'incomer' to the village from Wishaw. He and I soon made many new friends and funnily enough our next closest pal was also named Grant, Joe Grant. So, there were three of us - Gerry Grant, Arthur Grant and Joe Grant. All living in the same small village yet none of us actually related! It didn't happen, but I'm sure had we been apprehended by the police for any misdemeanour, the polis would have thought we were 'At it'.

Another of my pals was a boy called Willie Sinnet, he was the same age as me and he had a very mischievous sense of humour.

At Halloween each year we would get dressed up, usually as old women, go around the doors and if we were allowed in the house we would perform our party piece, sing a song or recite a poem. Then we would be rewarded with an apple or monkey nuts or a penny caramel. If we were lucky we got money, 3d, or if we were really lucky… 6d. One year Willie and I came up with the idea of going on to the bus from Calderbank into Airdrie. I would go upstairs and Willie downstairs, we would sing a song then go round with the collection hat. The conductress didn't even ask for the fare and we collected a couple of shillings for our effort. When we got to Airdrie we would get on the next bus back to Calderbank and repeat the exercise with Willie this time going upstairs. We did this for a few return journeys and it resulted in the most lucrative Halloween we ever had.

There used to be a Western SMT bus garage in Calderbank and occasionally there could be a change of drivers or conductresses at that depot. The staff coming off would go into the garage and there could be a few minutes delay for the staff changeover.

On other occasions, there would be an actual change of bus at the Calderbank depot and the conductress would shout "All change new bus" and the passengers would get out and transfer into another bus.

Willie and I were passing the bus stop at the depot one day and a Western bus was standing there. Willie saw the conductress and driver going into the garage, as he passed the entrance to the bus he shouted loudly "All change" then we both swiftly moved on. We looked back and watched the passengers streaming off the bus. We thought it would be safer at that point to make ourselves scarce. I would imagine there were a few disgruntled passengers and an even more disgruntled conductress.

THE STEEL WORKS

Calderbank in the mid 19th century was a prosperous village with a population of about 3500 and revolved around the iron and steel industry.

The Monkland Canal had been extended to Calderbank around 1800, the original iron company was taken over by a steel company who later made the hull plates for the 'Vulcan' - the world's first iron hulled passenger boat which was built in Scotland - and was launched in 1819.

The 'Vulcan' was actually constructed at Faskine, just about a mile from Calderbank, on the banks of the Monkland Canal. In 2014, a full-scale replica of the Vulcan arrived at Summerlee Museum of Scottish Industrial Life in Coatbridge.

The last time I drove through Calderbank, I noticed that the large Welcome sign to the village featured 'The Vulcan' … very appropriate indeed.

Airdrie, Coatbridge and the Monklands area had numerous iron works and as the iron industry in Scotland died the steel industry took over. The small, and seemingly insignificant, village of Calderbank can actually boast of having the first purpose built steel works in the country. Smelted and rolled steel were produced in Calderbank, and the steel ship plates for the Cunard Liners, including the Queen Mary, came from Calderbank. The steel works closed down around 1930. It was about twenty years after this that I came to the village and the old steel works were derelict. The population in 1950 was down to about 2,000 as many had left Calderbank and The Faskine to go to Corby in Northamptonshire, England, to follow the steel industry. Very many families from the Monklands area and other parts of Scotland descended on Corby, which was a small village before it was chosen as the site for Britain's biggest steel works. So much so that Corby inhabitants spoke with a Scottish accent for more than two generations. Many of the inhabitants of Calderbank had relatives in Corby.

The site of the old works area alongside the river Calder was always referred to as 'The Crusher'. I didn't question why but assumed that it was to do with the long gone steel industry. It was a popular place to play, in fact on recollection, it was a dangerous area especially when the river was fast flowing after heavy rain.

There was a precarious crossing of the river to take a short cut to reach the adjoining 'bigger sister' village of Chapelhall. This shortcut was at the foot of a street named 'English Row', a row of houses on a very steep dirt track road with the houses only on one side.

I imagine that before any council houses were built in Calderbank, the village basically consisted of Main Street and English Row and another street called Welsh Row.

At the bottom end of Main Street however, was what was known as 'The Square', or to be more precise, 'The Old Square' and 'The New Square'. I would imagine that these homes, if you could charitably define them as such, were built to house the iron-workers, in the early 1800's.

Each square consisted of two rows of two story tenements, one row on Main Street and a parallel row on Fir View. On the other side of Fir View it was all Local Authority houses.

The upstairs flats of 'the squares' were reached by ascending open staircases at the rear and many of the steps were damaged or insecure or had broken iron railings. The backyard area between the rows measured about 50 yards with many iron clothes poles to hang out the washing. In the centre of this common area was a small 2ft high walled square area, about 10ft x 10ft.

At two opposite ends of this was a wooden hut, which was in fact the two outside toilets for use by all residents in the square. There was no running water and the 'toilet' consisted of a plank of wood with a circular hole. I think it was only the Old Square that had this midden, the New Square had a number of outside water closets shared by all the residents.

To be honest, I think most people used some sort of commode or pails in their homes and just dumped the human waste in this walled area.

I remember someone telling me that one old man, who always used the outside dry toilet, had heard that the new council houses being built had inside toilets, he was disgusted at the thought of anyone "Doing a shite inside the house".

Most homes in the Old Square had no running water and drew their supply from a tap in Main Street. Neither did they have electricity or even gas in many cases. Lighting was by paraffin lamps or candles.

Cooking was done on the old fire grates. The new square, I think, had at least gas mantles for lighting and I suppose many had a form of gas cookers, but they too did not have electricity.

Everyone had coal fires in their homes and all the ashes would be dumped, along with the human waste, in the small walled areas.

At regular intervals, probably every fortnight or every month, there was a contractor employed by the County Council to empty all this rubbish. I think it was a person called Chalmers who had this job and he used a horse and cart for the collection. I can still recall watching him shovelling the shit and ashes into his very high cart. I would watch from a safe distance, the putrid stench got worse as he disturbed the contents of the dump. I thought then, 'God, what a shitty job that is'. Now, that should have been sufficient incentive to get a good education and avoid employment in any such like occupation... but was it?

I very quickly got to like Calderbank, as unlike High Street in Airdrie, there were a lot of green spaces, woods, a river, a canal, a football park and lots of places to go for a walk. Going for a walk and playing football, or 'headers', was almost entirely our only recreational activity.

It was a relatively small village where everyone seemed to know one another, which meant that our family were 'incomers'. You were required to live there for at least a generation before you were considered otherwise! That didn't bother me and I quickly enlisted a wide number of pals.

I continued to attend St. Margaret's Catholic primary school in Airdrie as it was the final year of my primary school education, but almost all the other catholic boys and girls went to St Aloysius School in neighbouring Chapelhall.

At that time, there was no catholic school in Calderbank but through attending Mass, church services, by being in 'The Boys Guild' and other communal activities, I had lots of friends.

The village also had its share of characters and almost every boy, or man, seemed to have a nickname. I recall that I thought some were rather strange; 'scone', 'squib', 'wee boy', 'snapper' and many more. It was here I first became aware of a 'homeless person'. This person lived in the nearby woods and he would call occasionally at certain homes (I believe his parents or relatives) to get food and I suppose occasional clothing. Although he presumably could have lived with his family, he chose to live in the woods.

One of Calderbank's 'characters' was a very likeable and truly well loved man who was, well I suppose, just a bit simple, that's how we would describe him then. Johnny Hughes, he could not read or write, he was not employed but by gosh he could work, going messages, digging gardens and all kinds of odd jobs.

He loved to walk and was always on the road. He also loved to sing, he would almost get the tune right but totally mixed up the words, or made up his own, and they never made sense.

If someone was sending him on an errand to Airdrie they would give him his bus fare but Johnny would walk there and back and so save the money. He seemed to spend all his earnings on 'McCowans Toffee'. Newhouse Industrial estate was just a mile or so outside Calderbank but Johnny would give that site a wide berth on his walks. "Naw they would pull you in and give you job" Johnny would say.

The Parish Priest, Father Michael J Dooley, was also a great local character and Johnny of course was one of his parishioners. However, Johnny said he always tried to avoid meeting him in the village in case he asked him to go somewhere for him. "He never gives you any money for going" Johnny said.

Johnny would visit our house regularly and enjoy a cup of tea and some of my mother's home baking. We would also have many sing songs at weekends and he liked to join in, in his own inimitable way, of course we would give him a few three-pennies for his efforts. He liked to be paid for his chanting and he could buy more candy, which cost three-pence a bar.

Frank Gallagher's Shop - 'Open all Hours'

There was a TV series called 'Open all Hours' in the 1970s but theterm 'open all hours' could be applied to Frank Gallagher's shop in Fir View Calderbank, in the 1950s. Frank and his brother Eddie ran the shop, which sold all kinds of goods; cigarettes, sweets, tinned foods, bread, scones, tea-bread, lemonades, firewood (bunches of sticks), tea, sugar, fly catchers, soap, bleach, and lots more. His, however, was the most peculiar shop in that he kept almost all of the merchandise in his bedrooms 'through the back'.

The front shop was very spacious, behind the long broad wooden counter he had many shelves, but most of them were empty. Perhaps he didn't trust people, or maybe he didn't want to put temptation to steal in their way.

He had a display window shaded by a kind of net curtain and two or three shelves in the window. All that he placed here was some scones, tea-bread, loafs of bread (unwrapped and unsliced). Nothing else was displayed in the shop window. That should have been his 'point of sale' advertising aid, but Frank, I'm sure, didn't attend any marketing course.

It was an experience to shop there! You would ask for, say, a tin of beans and Frank would shuffle through to the back and return with the tin, then you would ask for a bottle of Irn Bru and he would shuffle through once more, "and ten Woodbine Frank", he'd come with the Irn Bru and then go back through for the cigarettes.

I'm sure he must have been capable of remembering two items at a time but he seldom seemed to put that ability into practice. The real classic example though was when you asked him "What kind of sweeties have you got Frank?" The answer was always the same: "bilins" The colloquial pronunciation for 'boilings' or boiled sweets such as soor plooms, candy striped balls, mint humbugs etc.

Why he never displayed his candies in jars on the empty shelves was a mystery to all his customers. A small queue of three or four customers could take an eternity to be served, he must have covered many miles every day and worn treads in the wooden floor.

There wasn't much choice however of shopping elsewhere, unless you walked up to the top end of the village or 'Maggie Reids' sweetie shop half way up.

The 'open all hours' aspect is exemplified here... when some men on a Saturday night would be coming off the last bus from Airdrie, leaving at 12 midnight to Calderbank, and they needed matches or cigarettes, they would knock Frank's door or window until he came out in his nightwear and they would shout through the door their requirements. "A box o' matches Frank" and without a word of acknowledgement Frank would eventually appear at the door with the matches.

Frank never seemed to smile very much and his brother Eddie was the very opposite, he was always smiling and laughing. Eddie seldom served the counter however and perhaps that was the reason for the opposing natures. Frank got all the shuffling to do.

The only time we ever saw Frank outside of his shop was on a Saturday night when he was dressed all in black in a long coat with a velvet collar. Immaculately dressed to attend the Saturday evening vigil mass at St. Margaret's Church in Airdrie.

Frank of course was Irish or of Irish descent as was most of the catholic population of the village, either first, second or third generation Irish. As such, Irish tradition was practiced in most catholic families and one of the traditions was to buy 'The Irish Weekly' newspaper. I recall I always went straight to the column which each week published the words of some Irish song or ballad. I would cut it out and keep it safe in a notebook, I had a collection of hundreds of Irish songs. I still have some of these cuttings to this day... but as my wife Rena says "you're a hoarder" and I admit that is so.

My excuse for this refusal to throw anything out stems, I'm sure, from the fact that I was born just prior to the start of World War II and so for the first twelve or so austere years of my life we were on rations! Most families just scraped by on food. Many times, my mother would give me a cup saying "Go'n down to Mrs Magilton's and ask her for a cup o' sugar for your mammy".

There was little or no means of buying any luxuries. Toys were a luxury and the only toys I had was a box of lead soldiers! I also made toy guns by joining two clothes pegs together using my imagination. I spent hours playing on the floor with my toy soldiers. Today of course, using lead in toys or in paint is against the law and rightly so.

We were blissfully unaware of the danger of lead and many a time I would have these soldiers in my mouth. Another source of injecting lead into me was sucking the rain drops from the painted railings on the outside staircase of our house when we lived in High Street Airdrie. I don't know why I did it, young boys didn't need reasons for doing what they do. I can still remember the taste of the lead from the raindrops, although I didn't think of it as lead at that time, it was just the taste of the rainwater. All our water pipes then were also lead pipes so maybe it tasted much the same as the water from the tap.

To get back to Frank Gallagher and 'The Irish Weekly', this newspaper carried a regular appeal for money for the Missionaries. They asked everyone to save their 'Bun Pennies'.

A bun penny was one which had the young Queen Victoria head on the coin, her hair was tied in a bun, hence the name. Victoria was on the throne so long they had to change the head on the coins to depict an older version of the monarch.

The newspaper offered a prize of a watch, not a gold one I'm sure, for the person sending in the most bun pennies during each year. Frank won that watch on more than one occasion, putting Calderbank on the fundraising map.

FR. DOOLEY

Father Dooley, a big jovial Irish priest, was the first priest to the new parish of Corpus Christi, Calderbank, and he certainly was a special character. He would walk the streets of the village reading his breviary dressed in his long black clothes and usually wearing a biretta, a custom that few priests wore out on the streets, by the 1950s. As young boys, we avoided him in the street, as he would catch you by the arm and hold on to you so that you were going wherever he was. He would talk constantly to you and say repeatedly "Ah, yer a good boy, yer a good boy", as though he were talking to an obedient dog. He would let go your arm only when he reached his house, you weren't free until then.

Mass was said in Latin in those days and Fr. Dooley could say the mass in about 15 minutes, but when he started the sermon he could talk for an hour. Sometimes his broad Irish accent made it difficult to understand him. He was good at getting people to do work and raise funds for the new church that was to be opened in 1952.

He expected every catholic tradesman and labourer in the village to give freely of their time to build the hall and he was very successful in this project. A few years after the church was opened a lovely parish hall was built using this volunteer labour, and many a good dance we had in that hall.

There were many stories of his escapades and I believe most were true. It was an experience going to confession to Fr. Dooley. You often thought that he just wasn't listening to you, in fact I'm sure he wasn't most of the time. He would interrupt you when relating your sins, sometimes more than once with "Have ye ever in yer past life disobeyed yer father or yer mother?" or if it was a Saturday as it usually was "How did the Celtic go today, did they win?"

There was one particular young woman who did a lot of work in the church, she no doubt had very few, or probably no sins to confess. After she came out the confessional, Fr. Dooley would sometimes open his door and shout after her "Yer a saint Mary, yer a saint". He invariably opened his door to see who was coming in which was a bit disturbing really. However, he never opened the door after I left to tell me I was a saint!

His seating for the new church came from County Meath in Ireland. That must have cost a fortune, even for just the transportation, he was very proud of his seating. When kids knelt down on the kneelers their mouths were at the level of the backs of seats in front of them. As kids do, they put anything in their mouth, so their teeth were damaging the seats with lots of teeth marks. He would complain bitterly during his 'sermon' saying, "you children stop eating my seats, do ye hear".

Before he came to Calderbank he was a curate in St. Patrick's Coatbridge for about 21 years. We heard stories of how he would go round the snooker halls in the town with a stick that he carried. It could be in May or October when all the Catholic churches would hold Devotional Services on some evenings of the week. He would threaten all the young lads and men waving his stick saying "Come on, get up to the chapel for October Devotions instead of this den of iniquity". Some of the men he was speaking to of course were not Catholic.

"We're not Catholics Father".

"It doesn't matter... It'll do you no harm", was his response.

He also used to look after the Boys Guild football team in Coatbridge, and was constantly getting into trouble with the organisers for throwing stones at his players and running on to the pitch giving his boys instructions. They were threatening him with being banned.

"It's my park, I'll do what I like", he would reply.

Despite all his foibles he had a heart of gold and in most cases, was dearly loved by his parishioners.

It was around 1949 when we moved into the flat in Main Street Calderbank. This house did have electricity and gas cooker, but no inside toilet or bath. There was an outside toilet, with no door, at the rear of the backyard but it was only used for a pee, if you happened to be out in the yard when the need arose.

We had a large cupboard, or 'press' as it was called, where we kept brushes and shovels, hung coats etc. and in there we had a pail to use as a toilet. There was also a 'potty', which I suppose my mother would use before depositing in the pail. This pail of course was never allowed to remain any length of time in the 'press' when deposits were made therein, so the job of emptying it outside into the small walled area behind the outside toilet, usually fell to me. I hated that with a vengeance. Mostly we would use the public toilet in Crowwood Road, even though there was always a horrible smell in that toilet and it was filthy! Public toilets in those days were really smelly, dirty places. This small dump area in the backyard contained all the emptied pail deposits and ashes from the fireplace, plus any other trash. Any waste that could be burned such as newspapers or food wrappings, anything that was flammable was burned in the fire and converted into ash. So basically, the dump area contained only human waste and ashes and some empty tins and jam jars. We had by then stopped returning empty jam jars to the Co-operative stores to get a halfpenny for the 1lb. jar and a penny for the 2lb jars.

This small dump area was understandably very smelly, especially in summer. When the refuse was due to be removed by the person commissioned by Lanarkshire County Council, there was a problem. You see there was no entry to our backyard except through the narrow close, so his horse and high cart could not get through. I doubt if the man was prepared to shovel barrow loads and wheel it out to the Main Street and again shovel it up on to the cart. His answer was to take the horse and cart to the adjacent premises on the other side of the six feet wall separating the two back yards. He then shovelled the shit and garbage throwing it high to leap over the wall and hopefully into the cart.

As was fairly common in most villages in the West of Scotland, there was a 'pitch and toss' school. The local men would gather in a wide circle and in the centre one man would toss two pennies in the air spinning and turning all the way. The men would be betting on how the coins finished on the ground, either heads or tails. I don't know the rules, I never indulged in pitch and toss but it was a popular betting game and widespread I think, especially in mining areas.

The village had two locations where this illegal gambling took place, in areas where they could make a hasty retreat if the police made an appearance. One was down near the canal sluice and the other was near the top of the town at a point known as the 'three corners'.

It was funny to watch all the men's heads following the coins up in the air and then down to the ground as though they were bowing their heads in prayer, which reminds me of the story I heard of a foreigner visiting Scotland on a train, and witnessing pitch and toss schools which were often situated near railway lines. He thought Scotland was a very religious place with all these circles of holy men bowing their heads in reverence.

We had only lived in the Main Street flat about two years when we had the opportunity to swap houses with an elderly lady, who had a five apartment council house in Fir View. She was living on her own as all her family had moved away and the house was too big for her. She agreed to the swap and the County Council authorised it. It was pointed out to the old lady that there was no inside toilet.

"Ach, I was aye well used tae sittin ma erse ower the wooden hole" was her response.

So, about 1951 or 1952 was the first time I lived in a house with a toilet and bath, my boyhood dream was realised.

MY MAMMY

I have already covered my memories and experiences with my father and I had some criticisms of his parental responsibilities, or lack of them. Most of his transgressions occurred when I was too young to fully comprehend them, in addition to the fact that I really didn't see too much of him in my young days but it was the exact opposite with my mother.

One's mother is every child's first love and protector and she certainly was mine. I suppose most people will consider their mother to be one of the world's best and so I make no apology for ranking her in that category whilst being aware that I am probably a little biased.

Whilst I had many reservations about my father, I had none about my mother who showered me with love. We didn't call her 'mother' or 'mum' of course. In those days, in Airdrie, she was always called 'ma Mammy'.

She had it quite tough considering my father's nature and drinking habits. As I am the youngest in the family I cannot comment on how things were in the early years of the marriage but my sister, the oldest in the family, no doubt saw how things were at an early stage and I take her word that she witnessed, and endured, much more than I could have imagined.

I think my mother found some solace at her own mother's house in Kippen Street, Coatdyke and probably spent much more time there than would normally be expected.

That meant that I also spent a great deal of my early years at 'my Maws', we called our granny 'Maw' and our grandfather, 'Da'. I'll speak of them and their house later.

Having been born just before the second world war started there was a great deal of austerity in my early life, so money, or rather the lack of it, was a constant problem.

I believe my Maw helped my mammy out a great deal in providing the necessities that my father neglected to do. He would rather spend it on alcohol.

My mother, naturally, spent a great deal of time, cooking, cleaning and baking but in addition, a great deal of knitting.

I must admit that a spotlessly clean house was not her first priority. Of course she did her housework, cleaning, washing, drying etc. but to be honest it was more of a make do and mend affair. Let's be generous and say that our house in High Street could best be described as 'lived-in', as opposed to being a show-house.

A housewife's work in a tenement flat in the 1940s was certainly no 'piece of cake'. As described earlier there were no domestic appliances to make life easier. Married women with children did not go out to work because running a house and family in the conditions they lived, was in itself a full time job.

The coal fire was the only source of heating in the kitchen, which, in effect, was actually the living room, cum-dining room, cum-bedroom (I could not get out of the habit of calling the main living room of the house 'the kitchen', whichever house I was in. Many years later when we bought our first home in Irvine, a 3-bedroom semi, McTaggart & Mickel home, my wife would reprimand me for occasionally referring to 'the lounge' as 'the kitchen', old habits die hard).

Occasionally, some cooking or boiling of kettles was done on the fire range. Coal fires created a lot of dust and stoor giving extra work in cleaning. The range itself had to be black-leaded and 'silvo' polished. Washday was in effect almost a full days work, as described earlier.

Then there was the drying and the ironing, no electric iron but one that had to be heated on the gas stove, spit on it to see if it was hot enough, or not too hot. When it was too hot your sample spit would sizzle and bounce off the iron at speed and you hoped it missed your wrist.

When we got our first council house (with an inside bathroom, I add with pleasure), my mother acquired a gas-fired washing machine. This was a free- standing machine consisting of a tub with a hand-operated agitator to scrub the clothes. You filled the tub with water and lit the gas underneath to heat the water. It had a wringer attached. It was warm and exhausting work, so my mother used to get me to do the hand agitating and I would strip to the waist when performing this sweaty work.

Mothers had to find time to go for the shopping and that meant going to several shops. There were no one-stop-shopping supermarkets, so she had to visit the dairy for milk, the greengrocer for vegetables and potatoes and fruit, a grocer's shop for general foodstuffs, the ironmongers for hardware and cleaning materials, soap bleach etc.

The nearest thing to a supermarket was the Co-operative Store but they also had separate shops for butchery, bakers, drapery etc.

There were no fridges and freezers, so basically you were shopping for each day otherwise milk would turn sour. Oh God, I hated sour milk, the smell would make me boke. On a hot summer day milk would 'turn' very quickly and often was kept in a basin of cold water to make it palatable a little longer.

Some people could actually drink sour milk and I remember my mother and brother Jim quite liked it, Boke! There was also a sour milk cart, a horse driven cart with a barrel of sour milk, which occasionally could be seen in the streets. I think sour milk was mainly used for baking and that's certainly what my Mammy used milk that was 'on the turn' for.

BAKING AND KNITTING

Baking… and my mother were synonymous. Everyone loved her baking, her specialty was her apple tarts. Oh, even as I write this I can still smell them, also her soda scones and her sponge cakes and fairy cakes, what they call cupcakes now.

This reminds me of when I was doing my National Service in the Royal Army Pay Corps in 1958/60 and being paid a mere pittance, we were always hungry for tasty bites.

My mother would occasionally bake some fairy cakes and pack them in a Kellog's corn flake box and post the parcel to me in Newcastle-Upon-Tyne, where I was stationed. The other boys in the billet knew this parcel and when it arrived they gathered around me for the opening of it. They eagerly devoured the contents in no time at all, but I always managed to retain a few for my own personal pleasure later. The lads regularly enquired "Is it not time yer mammy sent ye some mair o' they cakes?" Sadly, I never seemed to be on my own when the parcel was delivered.

Apart from her baking skills, my mammy was the most incredible knitter I have ever known. Any spare time she had was spent knitting but not just any kind of knitting, she was an expert at knitting the complicated 'Fair Isle' patterns. I can picture her sitting with her two needles connected to about seven or eight balls of different coloured wools. I was amazed at the beautiful patterns and designs she accomplished. All of these patterns were in her head once she had looked at the paper pattern. She also made her own patterns. Her ability to conjure up such phenomenal works of art in her 'Fair Isle' patterns I found awesome and quite incredible.

She knitted slipovers and jerseys for all the family and also used the sewing machine to make articles of clothing. I remember she made me a pair of trousers (I was always in short trousers until I left school at 15 yrs. old) and a jerkin out of an old Army blanket. I hated that outfit, the material was thick and rough at the hems of the trousers, just above the knee. It rubbed against my legs and made them scurvy, red and itchy. It was worse when they got wet with rain.

In addition to scurvy legs above the knee, I managed to get them scurvy also just below the knee where the top of my 'wellies' rubbed against my legs. I just hated wet weather and there was no shortage of that in Airdrie.

I seldom wore wellingtons, my feet were always cold in them. I didn't wear shoes either as a child… the normal footwear for me was 'tack-ety-boots'. Black leather boots with steel toes and heels with tackets all over the sole. They were great for sliding especially when there was a covering of frost or slight snow.

I remember the sloping playground at St. Margaret's primary school and the slide we made. The more we all slid down the more it became like a sheet of ice and widened as it got near the bottom beside the boy's toilets. It then became a bit treacherous to walk on and it was fun to watch so many landing on their bum.

Apart from the normal daily wearing of boots, I always, in the sum-mertime, had a pair of sandshoes, or as we called them 'gutties'. When I put them on they were so light compared to the heavy boots, I just wanted to run and run… and I could in those days.

I was an expert at running along the sloping tops of the stone dykes that separated the backcourts of the tenement flats in Kippen Street Coatdyke. These dykes were about six feet high so if you fell off you could do yourself a bit of harm. I can honestly say that despite running at speed along these dykes, I never once fell off. I had good balance then.

I also remember the rows of brick built back-to-back coal cellars with concrete roofs, which were also about five or six feet from the ground. At the far end of the coal cellars there were two washhouses and these also had concrete roofs. We were always climbing trees, walls or any-thing that gave us a challenge. The distance between the wash houses and the coal cellars was probably about six or seven feet but the wash houses were much higher, probably about nine feet high, so if we felt brave we would jump from the wash house roof to the coal cellar roof, then brag of our daring to those afraid to try the high jump.

Another of my mother's famous knitting achievements were the Aran sweaters. These were made popular by the Clancy Brothers and Tom-my Makem in the late 1950s and early 60s, if you Google some imag-es of their albums you will see them wearing their trademark sweat-ers. I really loved the one she made me with the cable stitch pattern.

There were various styles of stitching giving a completely different look to the sweater and different neck styles. The wool I believe came from the Aran Isles off the west coast of Ireland and not the Scottish Isle of Arran (with 2 'Rs'). This wool yarn retained its natural oils (lanolin) which made the garments water-resistant and meant they remained wearable even in wet weather.

I had great wear out of that sweater, until it was washed in water that was too hot, it shrank in size and became very thick. Sadly, I could no longer wear it.

Just before I was married my mother knitted me an 'all over' fair-isle jumper. That means it did not just have a fair-isle border around the v-neck but had the fair-isle pattern all over the jumper. It would take much longer to knit and was quite a complicated piece of work. I think all her granddaughters had a fair isle knitted beret. That meant she knitted 21, as the other 15 of her 36 grandchildren were boys.

There's no doubt that knitting was my mother's favourite occupation. She also had a circular knitting machine, which could knit stockings and scarves and did so in a remarkably short time.

The heels and toes of course took a little longer to negotiate. She used to knit lots of woollen stockings for the nuns in the convent. A labour for which she wouldn't have received any payment, she wouldn't dream of charging the nuns. I think after we moved to Calderbank the circular knitting machine was no longer used. It would be difficult to describe this machine but Google images contains one something like my mother's and that photo brought back some fond memories.

The '100ᵀᴴ Birthday' Bash

This reminds me of a celebration we had to commemorate what would have been her 100th birthday. My mother was born on 9th July 1904 and died at the age of 71 in 1975.

Early in 2004 one of her granddaughters, Anne, who is of course my niece, was visiting us in Ardrossan and we were talking about my mother. It suddenly dawned on me that this year would have been her

100th birthday so it was decided there and then that we would have a '100th Birthday Party for Granny Grant', even though she had been dead for about 29 years.

In our large extended family, any excuse to have a family gathering and sing song was legitimate. All her remaining children, her 36 grandchildren and also many of her great grandchildren were invited to a party in St Edward's church hall in Airdrie.

The grandchildren were all asked to bring something that Granny had knitted or some present that she may have given them. Some of the 36 however, lived in far off shores, Australia, New Zealand, USA and Canada for a start, but most of them turned up on that July night.

Many of the girls still had their fair isle beret and wore it that evening plus some other knitted garments which were by that time a bit old fashioned but still worn with pride that night. We had a grand time reminiscing family events, and of course a few drinks, so it wasn't long before the singing began and some demonstrations of Irish dancing. I brought along two items that night, one was an old tin that had possibly contained chocolates or sweets when purchased. The tin commemorated the Visit to the Royal Burgh of Airdrie of King George V and Queen Mary on 9th July 1914.

As none of our family could be described as avid 'monarchists', I often wondered why my mother kept this tin and not discarded it, but one day it dawned on me... That date was my mother's 10th birthday. Perhaps it was a birthday gift, in any event she kept it and it is now one of my sentimental keepsakes.

The other item I brought along was a gold, or gold plated, umbrella handle end piece. Well that's what I think it was, it was engraved and had the date 9th July 1925. This date was of course my mother's 21st Birthday. Sadly, I did not see either of these items whilst she was still alive so could not ask her and therefore I just have to guess at the story behind them.

Because my mother spent so much time at my Maw's house in Coatdyke, I had as many or even more friends there than I had in High Street in Airdrie.

My sister's first house was a 'single end' in Deedes Street in Coatdyke. A 'single end' house meant just one room. One room that served as your living room, kitchen with a sink and cooker, and a bed recess. No inside toilet and considering she had three children there before she got a council house in Thrashbush, it was very crammed to say the least.

She soon filled the three-bedroom, Thrashbush house, with a total of nine children. This house in Thrashbush became my second home as I spent a great deal of my time there after school, going 'messages' for my sister or 'watching the weans'.

Very often she would say "On your way back go into Phil's café and get me some ice lollies". I didn't realize then, that pregnant women got cravings for certain things. Mary Therese, who was ten years my senior, had a craving for ice-lollies. Hardly a year passed without a new addition to her family, so, very many ice-lollies were consumed. I spent so much time there that some of my older nephews and nieces just called me 'Our Gerard' rather than uncle. This was not surprising as her oldest child was only about 11 years younger than me.

I mentioned earlier that I wouldn't accuse my mother of being overly house-proud. Very often things would be just shoved under the cushions of the chairs if she was trying to tidy up in a hurry, or if someone came to the door. It was mainly newspapers, comics or circulars, but it often took her a long time to get round to putting them where they should go.

In later years, when her heart condition discouraged her from climbing the stairs, she would often deposit items under the cushions, saying to herself 'I'll take them upstairs later' It would usually result in things being left under the cushions for days on end. She also suffered from a sore back and she had some kind of reinforced corset, her 'pink stays', which she would wear occasionally, and in the early evening she would remove it to give her some relief.

This operation would take place in the downstairs lounge and the corset would be on the sofa beside her until she was going upstairs. Our children reminisce now of the occasions they would visit their granny and find her pink stays under the cushion. They found this a source of great amusement and a little embarrassment and they still talk of granny's 'pink stays'.

Rena and I, with our four children, regularly visited and stayed over at my mother's house in Calderbank. Having six extra bodies in her two-bedroom house meant that my unmarried sister, Philomena, would share a bed with my mother, Rena and I had the second bedroom and the four children would fight for the best make-do beds on the sofa and chairs or sleep on the floor. We all knew we would have Granny's 'cheese and egg' for breakfast. This was a special dish, the technique of cooking it, I inherited from my mother. Even though I say so myself, everyone seems to love my cheese and egg. To this day, I get the job of cooking this specialty for breakfast anytime our family visit us. The rest of the cooking, to everyone's relief, is left to Rena.

My mother was always a very sociable person and liked nothing better than family gatherings. She also had been a nice singer in her young days and sang in the church choir. When she performed at home it was usually a rendition of 'Roses of Picardy', a song that was popular during the First World War. It was written by Frederick E. Weatherley, an English lawyer, author and lyricist who was credited of writing the lyrics of around 3,000 songs including the world famous 'Danny Boy. I think most people, like me, thought it was an Irish song.

Her social activities were mainly church related, she was a member of The Women's Guild and The Catholic Women's League but I don't think she went to the Bingo. She loved meeting people and talking, she had a heart of gold.

Living in a local authority house run by Lanarkshire County Council, there were occasions when the council workmen would be carrying out some repairs in the house, plumbing problems or some kind of building or joinery work. The council workmen were always happy to be visiting my mother as they were assured plenty tea breaks with scones and home baked cakes and she got to know a few of the workmen. A half hour job would always seem to require about two hours at her house. Her blethering to the workers, of course, prolonged the work no end. I wouldn't call her a nosey person but she was certainly… well let's just say, inquisitive.

The street she lived in, in Calderbank, was probably the busiest street in the village and most people had to pass her house at the beginning of the street. Being a fairly small village, most inhabitants knew, or knew of, one another. Her regular chair was facing out the lounge window and naturally she would see all those who were passing.

"Oh that's Mrs. So and So's daughter… where is she going… she's not at her work today".

"I hope her mammy's OK, she wasn't well last week" or "who's that man, I haven't seen him before".

We just let her rave on and took little notice of her comments on those passing by.

There was more than one occasion when she would notice some of the council workmen in the street, she'd think nothing of going to speak with them, see what they were doing, saying, "Well come in for a cup of tea when you're ready, I've baked some scones the day". No doubt they were happy to oblige.

I can still picture my mother sitting in her chair knitting away with several balls of wool leading down to the floor. When she had a cat, it would annoy her by playing with the balls of wool and Joey the budgie clinging on to the leg of her spectacles. We would lose count of the number of times she would nod off to sleep.

One of her favourite pleasures was to go on a 'bus run'. Didn't matter a toss where it was going, she just loved going for a bus tour. In later years when I had a car and visited her, I would sometimes suggest; "Do you fancy a wee run in the car somewhere". She was up putting her coat and hat on before I finished speaking.

I suppose everyone remembers their mother's common sayings and some that stand out with me are, "Do you think my name's Carnegie?" when I asked for something she could not afford.

Or if she had a meal ready for someone who was very late, "If he comes home alive, I'll kill him".

"Your no lookin' well, a clean shirt'll do ye";
"Your tea's only masking";
"Gaun yer dinger";

"He's got me up to high doh", were a few of her other sayings.

The only time I remember my mother having an actual job (no doubt she worked in the mills when she was a teenager) was when she worked at the Louis Speelmans clothing factory in Newhouse Industrial Estate. I know she was working there in 1952 as I distinctly remember the day King George VI died, 6th Feb 1952.
Because she was working, and not home till after 5pm, I had been given the regular duty after school, of peeling the potatoes for everyone's dinner. Now, the news of the death of the King was a big event in my mind so I did not peel the potatoes that day. I was out on the back green playing 'headers' with my pal Arthur when my mother got home and she shouted out the kitchen window.
"Get up here right now!"
I did of course, then I got what for!
"Why are these tatties not peeled, they'll all be in for dinner the now".
All I could think of as an excuse was, "But the King's dead", as though that would justify any action, or non-action.
"You'll be dead when I get a haud o' ye".
Well she got over it, she didn't slap me, in fact, I can never in my life recall my mother ever striking me. I put that down to me being a perfect angel… I'm also a good liar.

DID WE SEE HER ON A CRUISE?

I already said, when I picture my mother, it is usually a picture of her sitting knitting. Many years after she died, Rena and I were on a cruise on the Canberra cruise ship. The main function room on the ship held dances and variety shows and we were sitting there one evening enjoying some show. Just behind where we were sitting was the open-ended ship's library. Now we have cruised very many times but it's only very occasionally that you see women knitting on a cruise, there are too many other activities vying for their attention and participation.

At one point, I happened to turn my head round and looked in the Library. About 25 feet behind me I got a side view of a woman sitting knitting. The hairs on the back of my neck stood on end, literally.

I was sure I was looking at the ghost of my mother. Her build, her hairstyle and colour, her spectacles, her clothes, her very demeanour was the image of my mother. The only thing missing was joey not balancing on her specs. I trembled, shocked. I shook Rena and said, "Look behind you in the library".

Rena turned round and quickly brought her head back.

"Oh my God... Oh God... It's your Mother!"

We both sat there, took no more interest in the show on stage, I kept turning round, again and again and seemed more convinced with every glance that it was, indeed, her.

We were, in fact, terrified to approach and speak to her. I thought... "I'll go to the cabin and get my camera. No-one will believe me if I don't have proof."

By the time I got back to the ballroom the show was finished and everyone was making their way to some other venue on board. Most of those in the library had also dispersed and there was no sign of my 'mother'.

Now when you spend 14 nights on a cruise you will see almost all the passengers many times, even several times a day. Despite being goggle eyed searching throughout the remainder of the cruise, this woman was never seen again. I am very sceptical regarding the existence of ghosts, but this event made me wonder.

As I am writing this I remembered that our youngest daughter, Catriona (Cat), was on that cruise with us. She wasn't at the show in the ballroom, she was at a kids event. But I vaguely recall she had a dream that night.

Whilst I am writing this, my wife Rena was chatting on Facebook with Cat who now lives in Spain, so I decided to ask Cat, about this event, here is the transcript:

"Cat, can you remember when we were on a cruise on The Canberra when your Mum and I thought we seen your Granny Grant in the library, knitting?"

"Yes, I remember it well and think about it a lot".

I then said to her,

"How old were you then and next day, did you say you dreamed something?"

"Yes, I had a dream that night that my Granny was on the ship, I was about 12, I think. I told you at breakfast the next morning about my dream and I remember the amazed look on each of your faces when I said that. You hadn't yet told me about your sighting."

So, it gets curiouser and curiouser.

When I was about 12 or 13 years old I joined a new Scout Troop which was formed in Coatdyke, along with a few of my friends who lived in the area where my granny lived. I truly loved the Scouts, our troop was known as 126th Lanarkshire and 5th Airdrie. It fast became one of the best troops in the county having won, in only the second year from its inception, the annual, District and County competitions. There were many fund-raising schemes to gather in the much-needed cash to keep the organisation going and one was for parents to hold 'knitting bees'. That of course was right up my mother's street, as they say. So, she soon arranged one at our home in Calderbank, attended by a number of ladies doing their knitting.

The thing about that night, which I clearly remember, was the prank my father played on the guests. During the war years we were encouraged to be frugal and save on materials, one item we were encouraged to save was paper. Now this was a few years after the war but people still recalled the posters to 'save paper' amongst many other things.

As the night wore on and a few cups of tea consumed, the ladies would require a visit to the toilet. Each lady, on returning to the lounge after the toilet visit, seemed to engage in a fit of giggling, curiosity encouraged the others to visit the toilet to see the cause of the hilarity.

Unknown to my mother, my father had put a written notice above the toilet roll... 'Owing to the scarcity of paper, please use both sides'.

On the subject of toilet rolls, and going back to the 1940s, toilet rolls were an item that was not very much on the shopping list. We would always keep one, only to be put out when visitors... No... *special visitors*, were to arrive unexpectedly.

Instead of toilet rolls, most working class people used newspapers, cut or torn into squares of about six inches. A hole was pierced in one corner and the bundle tied with string and held on a hook beside the toilet seat.

Our newspaper of choice for this purpose was in fact the *'Radio Times'* as its pages were the right size to tear into quarters. If you were a bit more upper class and bought toilet rolls it would usually be *'San Izal'* toilet rolls. Now this roll of toilet paper was fairly hard and shiny and was impregnated, I think, with either Dettol or some other disinfectant. It certainly smelled like Jeyes fluid. It was more like greaseproof paper and I don't think it was fit for purpose. It tended more to smear rather than wipe your bottom. I recall one friend who likened it to John Wayne because "It was rough and tough and didn't take no shit" My mother had a cousin in New York, Anna Marie, she came to stay with us for a short holiday. She was amazed at this excuse for a toilet roll.

"That's greaseproof paper", she said.

"I wouldn't wipe my fanny with that".

It was then discreetly pointed out to her that a Scottish 'fanny' was totally different from the American version. She was so embarrassed when corrected but we all had a good laugh.

You could actually use *San Izal* as tracing paper and it was also very suitable as part of a musical instrument when wrapped round a comb. This was called a kazoo. You could make music of sorts with the paper and comb. I am not going to try to describe it but *'YouTube'* has a few examples of this comb music.

The aforementioned Anna Marie, a full cousin of my mothers, went with her parents and settled in America in the early 20th Century.

At the same time, I think it was in 1911, my grandfather went to America and found work in the iron and steel mills in Pennsylvania. He then sent for his family, that's my granny, my mother and her sister Mary and brother Hugh. They all landed on Ellis Island when my mother was seven years of age. New immigrants had to go through immigration control on the small island, before being granted permission to enter, live and work in the United States. Sadly, my aunt Mary was, well today we would say, had Additional Support Needs, so the authorities would not allow her to enter the country. So the whole family had to return to Scotland.

I remember as a very young boy seeing photographs sent from Aunt Anna Marie showing all her happy looking family playing in the snow in New York. It made me just a wee bit jealous of the clothes and toys and the home they lived in, compared to the austere conditions in post war Scotland.

Faith

As a family, we were fairly lucky regarding health and wellbeing, although my oldest brother died at age 9 months about nine years before I was born.

My brother Jim, four years my senior, did however develop rheumatic fever when he was about 11 years of age.

Rheumatic fever in the 1940s could often be fatal and in fact one of our cousins, Jim McGoldrick, died at age 16 so it was a very worrying time for the family as his life really was in the balance for a while and we were told that if he survives it could have an adverse effect on his heart.

As Catholics, we were of course aware of the apparitions of 'Our Lady of Lourdes' to Saint Bernadette in the French town of Lourdes. Many cures and miracles are attributed to the intercession of the Virgin Mary or St Bernadette at the grotto. Not surprisingly therefore any seriously ill catholic person would love to go to the shrine and hope for a miraculous cure. The cost of travel and care for a sick person to make that journey was well beyond the reach of our family at that time.

We attended St Margaret's Church in Hallcraig Street in Airdrie and the Women's Guild there raised funds to send one sick person to Lourdes each year. Our Jim's name was submitted to enter the draw to choose the lucky person to be sent to Lourdes and his name was drawn out the hat. There was great excitement in the house and we all thanked God, St Bernadette and Our Lady of Lourdes and every other saint we knew for guiding that hand in the hat to Jim's ticket. Although my mother was warned that the rheumatic fever could leave Jim with a weak heart and he would have to be very careful throughout his life, he went on to get married to Ellen and they produced no less than eight healthy children. He lived to the age of 67 and it was cancer that dealt the sad fatal blow in the end.

As a family, we could be described as faithful, practicing Catholics, especially my mother. Her faith was the most important thing in her life, after family of course.

One of my sister Mary Therese's sons and one of my brother Jim's sons both entered the seminary for the priesthood and the first one, Father Joseph Brannigan, was ordained a priest in 1978. Five years later Father James Grant was ordained to the priesthood in Calderbank. Two of my mother's other grandsons also entered seminaries, Joseph's brother John Brannigan preceded Joseph at Blairs College in Aberdeen but left after a short time. My brother Joe's son, Joseph, joined the Xavarian Missionary Fathers seminary in Coatbridge. He did become a deacon and served in missionary work with down and outs, homeless and drug addicts in Chicago. He didn't follow through to be fully ordained but he still works in various capacities within the church in Louisville, Kentucky USA.

There was great pride and celebration for the extended family with the first ordination of Fr. Joe Brannigan and I am not ashamed to say that I cried a few tears that day. Tears of joy at the event but also tears of sadness, that my mother did not live to attend that ordination.

Had she lived for only another three years she would have witnessed what would have been her proudest moment in life. I'm sure her heart would have burst with pride, as it would also have done when Father Jim was ordained. Oh, why did God deprive her of this great joy? She would just have said; "Its God's will, son".

A Heart-breaking New Year

Father Joe Brannigan was a popular priest in every parish he served and had a knack of getting parishioners involved in all the schemes he dreamed up.

In his last two parishes St Brigids, Newmains and St Marys, Lanark he was responsible for an enormous amount of refurbishment in the church and the halls.

He was also very fond of good social evenings and singsongs at his mother's and other family member's homes. His signature tune was The Homes of Donegal and he would enter the house singing 'I've just called in to see you all, I'll only stay awhile…'

It would bring a smile to everyone's face and usually they would join in the verses.

On New Year's Day 2014, he had his mother and a few other members of the family over to his home for a festive dinner. He went to bed that evening and died in his sleep. He was just a few days short of his 60th birthday. This was the most devastating thing that ever happened in the Brannigan and Grant families. It was unbelievable, unexpected and harrowing. At his Requiem Mass at St Marys there were three Bishops and over 80 priests on the altar and Father Jim Grant, his cousin, was one of the main concelebrants of the Mass. Both Jim and Joe had fed off each other during their priesthood ventures.

Father Jim delivered the eulogy in his own inimitable way and there was no one better qualified or more capable of doing so. In part of it, I recall he said "We would all like to think that Father Joe went to bed with his prayer book on the table, his rosary around his fingers, reciting novenas… Well, in fact he had a box of chocolates on the table and a large glass of a special malt whisky".

The church was overflowing and the service was broadcast to packed halls adjoining the church. He was buried in St Joseph's cemetery just a stone's throw from his mother's home in Airdrie. I penned a few verses to mark the occasion:

OUR DEAR FATHER JOE

The Good Lord called you Father Joe, at the close of the festive season
And though we try to understand, we'll never know His reason

As reality slowly edges in, Oh God, it's hard to bear
But we think of all the people in whose life you had a share

You touched so many lives, in, not just a spiritual way
But in guidance, help and effort and, just how many, who can say

The parishes you transformed not just in building restoration
But the hearts and minds you changed by your relentless dedication

You had a great advantage by the start in life you had
As part of a caring family raised by a loving Mum and Dad

Who instilled in you by example the importance of family life
And a faith and trust in God to cope with any strife

And that family's bound together, with love the major bond
A love that permeated from Joe, to everyone around

Though your name be Henderson or Davidson, the McCrorys or the Grants
We're all just one big family, We are all 'BranniGrants'

As, is our tradition, when we gather in our homes
It's never long till someone, starts the sing-a-long

And you'll be there in spirit Joe, singing with us all
No doubt you'll start as usual with 'The Homes of Donegal'

We'll follow that with 'Slievenamon' 'The Old Bog Road' and more
And not forgetting 'Skibbereen', That's always to the fore

In your short life, in many ways, you certainly left your mark
Not least the legacy you left St Mary's Church in Lanark

There are grieving hearts in every parish, wherever you did go
And all of us will say a prayer, for our dear Father Joe

MY SISTER PHILOMENA

My oldest sister, Philomena, at age 21 suffered a subarachnoid haemorrhage which I can best describe as a life-threatening type of stroke caused by bleeding into the space surrounding the brain. She did survive but had heart problems amongst many other ailments including her eyesight. Her heart problems meant she required a valve replacement to be inserted. Despite all her problems she unexpectedly lived until she was 76 years old.

She was the only member of the family who never married but always claimed to have "reared all her 36 nephews and nieces". She was indeed a character and she and her twin sister, Mary Therese, were truly like chalk and cheese.

Philomena was very much set in her ways, things were either right or wrong, no grey areas. She always spoke her mind, and said things as she saw them, even when her words could be interpreted as being offensive. She didn't really mean to offend and would be very upset if anyone did take umbrage. We all made allowances for her idiosyncrasies, difficult though it was at times, but nevertheless she had a heart of gold. I'm sure all her 36 nephews and nieces have a story to tell about their Aunt Philomena.

When Philomena was 20 years old and I was 10, she arranged, one Saturday, to have a day out to Ayr with one of her girlfriends. They would travel from Airdrie on the Western SMT bus straight through to Ayr via Hamilton, Strathaven, Darvel and Kilmarnock. There was a bus every hour on this service and the journey took about 2 hours 45 minutes each way. Now, I'm sure the two girls were looking forward to a day out to the seaside and maybe meet some nice boys, but my mother put a wee bit of a damper on their plans.

I was with my mother at my granny's house in Coatdyke, (Philomena had moved there to live with our 'Maw' at that stage) and she and her friend had just left to catch the 11am bus from Airdrie. I must have nagged a wee bit at my mother. "Why can I not go to Ayr, I want a day out too".

"Well, away you go, if you can catch that bus before it leaves she'll take you out for the day, tell her I said it".

I did manage to get to the bus a couple of minutes before it left so poor Philomena was stuck with me and she was not too pleased. Not surprisingly, the girls wanted to do their own thing and not be lumbered with a ten year old kid, so when we arrived at the promenade in Ayr, just beside the Pavilion, they told me to go on to the beach and walk down there (pointing southwards) and they would meet me near the end of the beach. That suited me and I happily strolled along the crowded beach, even paddling for a little bit.

Well I seemed to have been walking for quite a lengthy period and I could not see any 'end' to the beach and I thought, "God, maybe this beach goes all the way down to Girvan, when am I supposed to stop walking".

I began to panic and made my way up on to the promenade and walked back towards the Pavilion, eagerly scanning the many hundreds of day-trippers, looking for my sister.

It seemed like hours but probably was less than 90 minutes when we eventually met, near the place where we separated. There was a look of relief on Philomena's face but I assure you it was nothing to the relief this 10-year-old boy felt, and by the way, I don't think they met any suitable boys whom they no doubt were seeking.

SCHOOL DAYS

The old saying 'School days are the happiest days of your life', is no doubt true for many people. My experience and memories of school were indeed, mainly, very happy ones.

I am eternally grateful to the dedicated, loving, wonderful teachers we had in St. Margaret's primary school in Hallcraig Street in Airdrie. Miss Sweeney and Miss McGowan were in charge of the 'first babies', as the new 5year old entrants were known. I had Miss Sweeney, large in stature and full of love and caring kindness.

Other names I recall were Miss Fitzpatrick, Mr Curry, the wonderful Miss Tulip, Miss Heaney, Mr Shields, Mr Monaghan and Mr 'Paddy' White whose class was in 'the white house', a two room building totally apart from the main school building. I don't know whether it was so called after Mr White or because it was painted white, I think it was probably the latter.

I did not have 'Paddy' White as a regular teacher but I remember we went to his class one afternoon a week for some subject, which I cannot recall. What I do recall vividly, however, is that there were always extra bottles of milk in his class and they were offered to us and I would be first in the queue and often get more than one bottle. Each morning in each class, the teacher would ask how many children wanted the free milk and that number would be ordered. So out of a class of 50 or more pupils (yes there were classes with 50 pupils) maybe only 35 or so would ask for milk.

Paddy White did not ask if you wanted milk he just ordered one for every pupil. That is why there were spare bottles when we got to his classroom in the afternoon.

When I say bottles, these were very small about a third of a pint. Having been sitting in the milk crates all day they were usually very warm but that did not put me off. Throughout my life I have always loved milk.

Another teacher we had was Miss Gallagher, she always had a strong smell of tobacco smoke if you were near her. Of course we never saw her smoke but gauging by the smell I'm sure she would have been on over 20 a day.

There was also one other teacher who was a heavy smoker, Mr. Curry. We never saw him smoke either but the tell-tale signs of nicotine stained fingers was evidence of his habit. Similar stains to a lesser degree were also evident on Miss Gallagher's fingers.

Many teachers of course would have nicknames applied to them by the pupils. Mostly they were words rhyming with their surnames, like 'Smelly Kelly'. One name that stands out in my memory was a teacher called Mr McGeachy. You'd never guess… Aye, that's right, he was known as 'Keechie McGeachy!

I mentioned a class size of 50 pupils and this was common in our school. It was, after all, the only Catholic primary school in Airdrie and also served some other villages outside the town so class sizes were all very big.

I remember a school photo of our class taken in 1947 and I counted about 48 pupils in that photo. Bearing in mind that there were probably some absentees on the day of the photo shoot, perhaps we had over 50 in the class.

Forty years after that photo was taken, I got a call from one of the pupils who was attempting to have a '40-Year Reunion'. I got involved in the organising of the event which turned out to be very successful, it was well attended and also very enjoyable.

The function took place in St Margaret's Hall, the building which was the original small school in the 19th century and was used as the 'dinner hall' when I attended St Margaret's school in the early 1940s. This building was also used as a social hall for the parish and was referred to as 'The Canteen' where there would be 'men's smoker nights' and social functions. Many functions in our family were held there, birthdays, anniversaries and very many post funeral receptions. I always thought that St. Margaret's primary school buildings were quite modern looking, though on reflection I think it was the extensions that had been added that gave me that impression. The older part of the building had the boy's toilets situated in the basement, the cubicles without doors (or was there even cubicles?), did not have toilet pans, they had squat toilets.

These were just an oval shaped hole in the floor with a footprint at either side. You just did your 'job' kind of on your hunkers, hence the name I suppose squat toilets. I don't know if the girl's toilets were similar, I was never in them. The only place I ever saw squat toilets, many years later, was in the Far East, Thailand, Malaysia and Indonesia and I think they are still quite common there.

Just after the end of the war, when I was seven years old and rationing was still in operation, we used to queue for the butcher's shop across the road from where we lived in High Street. A number of boys were sent out early on a Saturday morning to 'keep the place in the queue'. This would be anytime from 7.30am and the shop didn't open until 8.30 or 9am. Naturally boys would get a bit bored so a ball was procured and we started a football game on the street.

Now that sounds a bit dangerous, playing football on High Street, but in 1946 there were very few cars on the road and horse and carts were still quite common. It became a regular match on a Saturday morning but some old busybody must have complained, as one Saturday, two policemen turned up and gathered us all together to take our names. We were nicked!

One of my brother Jim's pals was a lad called Iain Martin who was one of the team that Saturday, as was my brother Jim.

Iain had an unfortunate name, which lent itself to some poetic teasing and we used to shout at him (before we ran away), "Look at Iain staunin' peein', Look at Martin staunin' fartin'". In consideration that Jim was one of his close friends I didn't participate in these chants… well… sometimes.

Iain had an elder brother who had recently entered the local police service, he knew that his dad would be very displeased, to say the least, if he got into any trouble with the constabulary so he tried to make a getaway through a close. It was in vain however, as he was caught and presumably faced the wrath of his father.

I think it was the following Monday morning, fifteen of us all appeared in court in a long line facing the Justice of The Peace. I was the smallest and the youngest at the end of the line and the JP seemed to be sat quite high up at his desk. We got a stern lecture and a final warning that the football in the streets had to cease, we got off with just a reprimand. I don't think therefore, that this court appearance constituted a criminal record.

It was the afternoon before I went to school that day and Miss Fitzpatrick wanted to know the reason for my absence in the morning. "Please Miss, I was in the court".

After the story was related to the teacher with all the other pupils thoroughly enjoying it, the teacher was sympathetic, then they all had a wee laugh at my expense and were drawing sketches on the blackboard of the polis chasing the boys.

THE BELT, THE STRAP, THE TAWSE

Until the 1980s the form of punishment in Scottish schools was the leather strap or belt, sometimes called a tawse. We never called it the tawse, maybe the term was used in other areas but not in Airdrie. I was not aware of any schools using 'the cane', I thought it was only posh English schools that favoured that method of punishment.

Corporal punishment was officially abolished in 1987, but I understand it was not really used after about 1981 or 82. Roughly 30 years after I left school.

Now, I *'got the belt'* quite a number of times and I don't know why. I'm sure I was a perfect pupil and never did anything wrong... well that's how I remember it anyway. I cannot recall the belt being used very often in the primary school and I think it was reserved for more serious misdemeanours or gross misbehaviour. It was certainly a different story at the secondary school.

I mentioned Miss Heaney as one of my teachers, she had also taught my sister Mary Therese, ten years earlier. Now, she didn't use the belt much but all those who got their sums wrong were made to kneel on the knotted wooden floor while she chalked the correct answers on the blackboard.

On the few occasions I was kneeling there she would comment; "your sister never got a sum wrong in her life". I believe that was true and Mary Therese's brain is still as sharp to this day, at the time of writing this, she is approaching 90 years of age, has 18 grandchildren, 26 great-grandchildren and one great-great-grandchild. She keeps up to date with them all on Facebook! Probably by the time you are reading this, those numbers have increased.

Mary Therese had nine children, sadly one of them passed away just days before his 60th birthday. Big families are common in our connection but I'll cover that later.

My secondary school was *St Patrick's Senior Secondary School* in Coatbridge. There was not, at that time, a catholic secondary school in Airdrie. St. Patrick's catchment area therefore covered a very large geographical area including Airdrie and many villages around Airdrie, as well, of course, as the greater Coatbridge area. I remember some pupils in my class from as far away as Carfin, Salsburgh, Shotts, Caldercruix and Chapelhall. As a result, class sizes were much bigger in the early 50s than they are today and most classes had at least 40 pupils. I started mid term in January 1951 and because it was mid term I was put in to first year prep class. We had all the usual subjects plus French, Latin, Science etc. Classes were graded A,B,C,D,E,F, according to ability, so the smarter pupils were in *1A* and *1B* whereas

1C, 1D, did not get French and Latin and *1E* and *1F* were pretty low on the IQ table.

To get back to the subject of the *'belt'*, I was in class *1A* and one day the teacher who taught *1F* was off ill and we had to take a share of his class.

Our teacher had reason to belt one of the '*1F*' class pupils and was not pleased when the boy separated his hands before the belt made contact. After a few failed attempts the teacher was frustrated and I remember his words,

"Do you lot in 1F not know how to take the belt... Well here's what you do... Grant... come here and show them how to take the belt!"

I obediently approached the teacher, held out my hand and took the punishment in the recommended fashion. Then it dawned on me... I'm a right stupid eejit, but then again, disobeying the teacher had consequences too. To be honest he was very lenient with his strike.

Some teachers had a reputation for being very severe with the belt. One in particular was a history teacher and he did not give less than six strokes of the belt irrespective as to how serious the misdemeanour was. He carried his belt over his left shoulder and under his jacket, concealed but always at the ready. He came down with that belt with such great force, in fact both his feet left the ground when the belt was on the downward spiral. Your wrist often got a share of the leather and invariably resulted in great red welts on your wrist as well as your hands. He shared the six whacks with three to each hand.

The *Boys* and *Girls* playgrounds were totally separated at St Patricks. Each morning and after lunchtime break we had to line up in classes in the playground and be marched in to the building one class at a time. All very regimented. The duty of marshalling this entrance to the school building was mostly performed by a Mr Donnelly, 'Big Chuck Donnelly' as he was always called, by the pupils.

One morning when we had got into line the rain was coming down and we were anxious to get inside but Big Chuck was late in coming out to start the procession. A few frustrated pupils started to sing *"Why are we waiting, Why are we waiting"*
Very soon most of us were joining in.

I can still picture in my mind Mr Donnelly appearing on the top step at the entrance to the building, he looked around and then disappeared back inside. The singing continued.

Big Chuck then returned, but accompanied with six other teachers. Each pupil in each class was belted before they entered through the doors. Six or seven hundred whacks of the belt administered... that's a nice start to the day.

The sadistic history teacher looked especially pleased, glad I avoided him on that occasion.

The best exam results I had in the secondary school was at the end of the 6-month 'prep' term.

I was top for French at 86%, third top for Latin at 92% and was in the top three in every other subject, so naturally I went into 1A for the first year term.

After a year in *1A*, I was getting a bit lazy and wanted to drop Latin and French. I had to get a letter from my mother (my father was not living with us at that time) requesting that change to my education.

My two oldest brothers were doing their National Service in the RAF and the Royal Artillery so they were unable to influence my mother which I have no doubt they would have done and prevented me from dropping languages.

Going in to 2nd year I was put into class *2C*, as *2A* and *2B* did languages, however there was only 20 in that class and it was too small in number and was disbanded after only a few weeks and the class of *2C* transferred into *2A* or *2B*.

One sad thing about the disbandment of *2C* was that there were only five of us boys with the other 15 being girls, I liked that split!

I was put in to *2A* and once again got some of the teachers I had in first year. I remember the science teacher who gave me hell for dropping down. He made it very clear to me that I had the ability to benefit greatly from a good education and he was quite hard on me for the remainder of the term. I was determined however to leave school at 15 years of age and hopefully start as an apprentice joiner, which I never did.

I started 3rd year in August 1952 and as my 15th birthday was in November I left school at the mid term in December that year having only done two and half years of secondary education.

Oh how I regretted that in later years. The Science teacher was right, if only I had listened to him at the time. I had to get the remainder of my education from the 'University of Life'.

My married sister was ten years older than me and before I left school she had four children.

I spent a lot of time at her house and went for her 'messages' and did a lot of babysitting. I also often stayed over at her house, so much so that some of my nephews and nieces called me 'Our Gerard' instead of 'Uncle Gerard'.

I am ashamed to admit it but in my last six months or so at school I often played truant to be of assistance to my sister. Well that's the excuse I am making here but she would not ask me to stay off school. I was anxious to do so because she had a television which she got for the coronation of Queen Elizabeth and that was more interesting than schoolwork, although at that time TV programmes only started in the evening, there was no day-time TV.

Staying off school and watching TV, resulted, one weekday afternoon, in me having the privilege of seeing the great English National football team, including Stan Mortensen and Stanley Matthews, being beaten by 6 goals to 3 by the famous 'Mighty Magyars' of Hungary at Wembley stadium in November 1953.

This match became known as 'the match of the century' and featured Hidegkuti and Ferenc Puskas in the Hungarian team.

I marvelled at Hidegkuti's hat trick and the two goals from Puskas on a 12 inch black and white TV screen. Imagine, how jealous were my classmates when I was describing the wonders of these two 'gods'?

Another famous match I was privileged to witness on the 12inch screen was the Blackpool and Bolton FA Cup Final of 1953 which Matthews and Mortensen helped Blackpool to a 4-3 victory.

Whilst I regret 'doggin' the school (playing truant), I certainly don't regret seeing England getting trounced 6-3 by the Hungarians. A few years later, England humiliated and trounced Scotland at Wembley

by 9 goals to 3. Celtic's Frank Haffey was in goal for Scotland. The sarcastic joke that went around after that game,
"What's the time?"
"Haffey past 9".

MY MAW AND MY DA

Before you think I am talking about my mother and father let me point out that 'Maw and 'Da' was what we called our grandparents. I don't know where that tradition came from because in Scotland it was fairly common for parents, rather than grandparents, to be called Maw (or Ma) and Da. My brother John and his wife Sarah, were just as often called 'Ma and Da', as they were 'Mammy and Daddy'.

Both of my grandparents were born in the very early 1870s when Queen Victoria was on the throne and just a few years after the American Civil War. Having been born when they were, they both survived much longer than the normal life expectancy of people born in the 1870s. My grandfather died at age 75 and my grandmother at the ripe old age of 88.

I never thought that I, or any one of my siblings, would achieve that longevity but as I write this my sister is now 88 and my only other surviving brother, Joe, is 84 and I am 78, so we are getting there.

Probably… no… most definitely... my greatest fear and dread in life would be for any one of our children to die before me. I just do not believe I could handle that. I know how I felt when the first of my siblings, John, died of a massive heart attack and without any warning. Then my other brother Jim and sister Philomena died, not as suddenly as John, but it was every bit as painful.

With this in mind, in recent years I have often thought of just how my grandmother was able to endure the deaths of, I think it was at least six or seven of her children, most of them as babies, but one at 16 years of age and one at 50 years of age. Then, the death of her husband and later, in 1958, the death of her oldest son aged 60.

At that point the only member of her family that outlived herself was my mother. How on earth can anyone endure that number of family deaths and still remain sane? Life can be really cruel. I do not want to dwell on this subject so I'll quickly move on and pray that I will never encounter such suffering.

Only two of my grandparent's children, that is, my mother and her brother Hugh, were married, but the number of offspring of these two is nothing less than incredible.

My mother had seven children and 36 grandchildren. My Uncle Hughie and his wife Sarah also had seven children and 34 grandchildren. So in total my Granny had 70, yes 70 great grandchildren. Of course, she did not live to see all of them. I have not counted how many there were in 1962 when she died nor have I even tried to count how many Great, Great, Grandchildren there are now, there must be well over 150.

I spent a lot of time at my Maw's house and as a youngster occasionally slept there overnight. I just loved sleeping in the recessed bed, it seemed so much more comfortable than our recessed beds in High Street, Airdrie.

I was only five years old and just started school when my Da died in 1945. My memory of him was sitting in the big chair smoking his pipe and me running and jumping on his knee when I arrived at their house. I can still smell the distinctive odour of the Condor tobacco of his pipe and every time I smell it I think of him. He was a big strong man and worked as a 'puddler' in the iron works, an occupation that called for great strength, stirring the molten iron in the furnaces.

Their house in Kippen Street Coatdyke had a very small scullery, a living room with two recessed beds and a front room. That front room was out of bounds to all the grandchildren and it was only on special occasions that we were allowed in there, or when we were left in the house alone and did a bit of exploring.

There were no inside toilets in these three-storey tenement buildings. The three homes on each landing shared the loo situated on the half landing downstairs. No wash-hand basin, just a toilet behind a draughty wooden door. There was a nail on the door holding a bundle of torn squares of newspaper, which served as toilet wipes.

The staircase was lit by gas mantles, (when they weren't broken), but there were no lights at all inside the cludgie, so if you needed to go during the night you took a candle or just fumbled about in the dark.

The occupant of one of the houses sharing this toilet was an elderly spinster living in a 'single end', a one roomed flat. She was very fond of the monarchy and Queen Elizabeth had just recently come to the throne, so the newspapers, especially 'The Bulletin' and 'Picture Post' magazine, published a lot of photographs of the new Queen.

She actually pinned a newspaper cutting of a photo of "Oor Queen" on the inside door of the outside 'cludgie'. That, I thought, was a very strange act of loyalty of which I'm sure Her Majesty would not have approved. Shortly afterwards she complained bitterly to my Granny "Do you know what some bad rascal has done to the Queens picture in the toilet, they've pencilled a moustache on her".

I am sure she had little doubt of who the culprit was.

In the hallway of the flat, there was a massive iron mangle with two wooden rollers and used for pressing blankets or flattening sheets, towels and other laundry items. Can you imagine a monstrosity like that inside a modern day home? Or how it was carried up the stairs. That mangle took up a lot of space in the hallway but I cannot remember ever seeing my Maw use it but no doubt she did. I do, though, remember seeing her often spending a tiring day in the outside washhouse and she was still doing that until she was over 80 years old.

When she became unfit in her last two or three years she came to live with us in Calderbank, where life was a lot easier for her. The thought of putting her in a care home never entered our minds, people looked after their aged parents at home in those days and there was no 'care allowances'.

In our home she was seeing television for the very first time and I used to smile when at the end of some programme she was watching, the presenter would wave and say goodbye, she would politely return that wave to them and say goodbye.

After the war when sweets came off the ration we would always buy a box of *Black Magic* chocolates for her birthday but she never seemed to open them at the time. She would store them in the wardrobe in the front room and then months later she would open them when perhaps a few of us were there. Invariably the chocolates had all turned kind of white with age but we still ate them. That seemed to happen with every box of chocolates she was given.

MAW'S SPARE ROOM AND OUR 'OTHER BROTHER'

After the war in 1945 there was a housing shortage, most working class families rented flats or went on the waiting list for a council house. It was not uncommon for newly married couples to start off their married life in a room at their parents or even their grandparents home.

Our cousin Hugh McGoldrick (more often called 'Sonny' because his father was also Hugh) served in the Royal Navy during the war. He got married to Cathie in 1946, not long after he was demobbed and their first home was my Maw's front room until they got a single end flat just one floor up at the same address in Kippen Street. A few years later, my brother Joe and his wife May, lived in Maw's front room when they got married.

When Rena and I wed in 1963 we had a room in my mother's house in Calderbank for the first year, then moved in to a room at Rena's mother's house in Newarthill until we got a house to let in Irvine, but more about that later.

So whilst it was not the preferred start to married life there was really not a lot of options in the 1950s for newly weds who had not any substantial amount of ready cash or rich parents who could provide a deposit for a mortgage. Mortgage… I didn't even know the meaning of the word. Rena and I investigated the possibility of buying a flat and viewed one in Airdrie. The purchase price was almost £1,000. Good God, where would we get that kind of money? Nowhere, and even if a mortgage was explained to me, the banks only considered the husband's salary and not the wife's earnings.

To get back to cousin Hugh…

There was only one set of cousins on our mother's side of the family, the McGoldricks, and Hugh was the oldest of seven.

In our early days we were all fairly close, but as all the cousins were getting married and having families of their own, we didn't drift apart, but we saw a little less of each other, except for Hugh!

Throughout our lives, no matter what family event or celebration it was, weddings, christenings, parties, Christmas or whatever, Hugh and Cathie would always be there.

So much so, that we used to joke that Hugh was our 'other brother' rather than cousin. I am proud to say that my own six grandchildren are also all so very close that they treat one another as brothers and sisters. I am sure that feeling will prevail throughout their lives.

Now I would never, by any stretch of imagination call myself a poet, but I have throughout my life, written very many 'rhyming verses', mostly to commemorate a special birthday or anniversary or an event. I would normally try and bring a little humour into the prose and often would write in Scottish dialect, I found that much easier to do.

As I said, Hugh and Cathie got married in 1946 and so their Ruby Anniversary occurred in 1986 and there was a Ruby Wedding celebration in one of the local halls with a huge gathering of family and friends.

Needless to say all our family were there and I had prepared a few verses to mark the occasion. Cathie came originally from Armadale and had a guid Scots tongue on her and a plethora of Scottish sayings, so in deference to Cathie the verses were mostly in the local vernacular.

Before you read this 'poem' I will make you aware of one or two worrying incidents that had occurred.

Their eldest daughter as a very young girl was severely injured by the tyre of a bus while waiting to board the bus to take her home from school. I cannot remember what exactly happened but the tyre inflicted tremendous damage to a large area of skin on one of her legs.

She was taken eventually to Ballochmyle hospital in South Ayrshire and spent some time there getting skin grafts. It's a long drive from Airdrie to Ballochmyle for hospital visiting times.

The other incident was even more serious. It occurred on Glasgow Fair Friday 1973 as Hugh and his son Jim were in a small Austin Van Den Plas car. They had been collecting accounts regarding the milk business Hugh was operating at the time. They were involved in a head on collision by another vehicle, which I understand, was just coming out of a long bend perhaps at speed and strayed on to the oncoming lane.

Hugh was very seriously injured and for a few days things looked pretty grim. Jim, although injured, was much less critical. I contacted Jim in Austria recently to ascertain the injuries that he and his dad sustained. This was his response:

"My dad's rib cage was smashed-in by the steering wheel and a rib punctured one of his lungs, as the front of the car had been crushed back to such an extent that my Dad had to be cut out of the wreck using firemen's specialised equipment. The top of one of his femurs was fractured several times, possibly by the steering wheel. Consequently he had one leg that was about 4 inches shorter than the other one.

I don't remember how long he was in hospital but it was probably 3 or 4 months"

"I sustained a broken jaw which had to be operated on, and was then wired-up for many months in order to heal in the right position, during which I could only eat liquidised food. I also lost all of my front teeth."

"As soon as I got out of Canniesburn hospital, my brother Hugh took me in to see my Dad, as they thought that he might be thinking that I was dead.

However, the devastation of the impact of the accident was so great that my Dad could not even remember anything about his first month or so in hospital, nor could he ever remember anything at all about the accident"

"I was writing in my 'tick book' at the time of impact, I can only recall that my Dad called out "Oooh!" just before we were hit. As I had glass in both eyes, I was unable to help him in any way. The car itself was demolished beyond recognition, and when I went to see it a few weeks after the accident, strangely, but much to my Dad's relief, I found one of his dentures in the wreck"

Rena and I were living in Irvine at that time and my brother Jim and his family visited us to have a day by the seaside. I think we went to Troon for the day.

When we arrived home in Irvine we got the telephone message about the injuries of Hugh and Jim and a great anxiety and deep depression crept in and remained for several days until we knew that Hugh would survive.

Next morning, Fair Saturday, It was harrowing to see on the front page of the Scottish Daily Express a graphic picture of the mangled car with the headline 'Don't let this happen to you this holiday'.

That article really wrangled me and I felt a bit angry at the newspaper's headline which to me insinuated that Hugh was at fault. I felt that they were exploiting what to us was a very worrying personal family tragedy.

So here is the anniversary 'poem':
Written for the occasion of the Ruby Wedding
of Hugh and Cathie McGoldrick 26th April 1986

We're gaithered here tae celebrate, wi' Cathie and wi' Hugh
Their 40 years o' married life, tae each they've baith been true
On an April day in '46, an occasion of great joy
A bonnie lass frae Airmadale, wed her sailor boy.

They started aff in Kippen Street, at number 41
An Maw wis there when Hugh was born, They were proud o' their new son
Then they moved just up the stair, tae their ain wee single end
An' oan the next St Patrick's Day, Elizabeth came alang.

A bigger hoose in Elms Quadrant, gave them much mair space
An Hugh and Cathie did their best, tae increase the human race
Jim, Peter, John, Kathleen, Rosaleen and Tricia all arrived
Before they moved tae a better hoose, in classy Manor Drive.

An' if the weans did misbehave, or wandered aff the rails
A' Cathie wid hae to do, wis threaten tae 'floor their tails'
So now they've fower big handsome sons, the same number daughters
fair.
But I think we're safe in thinking noo, they'll no hae ony mair

Hugh cobbled shoes in Caldercruix, Calderbank and Holytoon
Efter that his laundry van, went all aroon the toon
An' then he wis yer pinta ma, up early every day
An' he finished aff his workin days in the hospital ower the way.

But they've had their share o' worries too, it wisny easy a' the while
An' I ken for sure they'll no forget, the road tae Ballochmyle
And nane o' us will e'er forget, the 13th of July
We prayed and prayed as ne'er before, and oor prayers were heard on
high.

And noo they've grandweans coming up, tae carry on the name
Some even oot in Austria, where they helped tae build Jim's hame
Who kens hoo many grandweans, in ten years time there'll be
When we're here again tae celebrate, their Golden Jubilee.

For us to say they are oor friends, is a privilege and an honour
Ye'll travel far an' never find, a better faither and a mother
So let's all charge oor glasses, wi' a toast tae Cathie and Hugh
An join wi' me tae say to them, … May God Bless baith o' you.

Ten years later it was of course their Golden Wedding and I really felt
obliged to pen a few more verses to update their life story.
I phoned Elizabeth, their oldest daughter, to give me some info on any
incidents.

THE GOLDEN WEDDING 1996

The last ten years has added six mair grandweans tae the clan
Four more girls and two more boys, make the total twenty wan
But anither generation has spread a branch o' the family tree
When their first great grandwean, Ross, was born in December 93

Every Saturday and Sunday, doon at Manor Drive
The grown weans and grandweans too, a' steadily arrive
Noo Hugh and Cathie know fine well, their hoose is no their ain
But that's the way they love it, the family know that hoose will aye be
'Hame'

But their living room wi' a' these folk, wis jist a wee bit sma'
So they jist took in a bedroom, by knocking doon a wa'
It wis a lot o' work and mess, and they grafted as a team
An everything wis perfect – aye even that damned beam

When Cathie and Hugh went ower tae Jim's, they stayed for 3 months
lang
An' I can vouch they were sadly missed, by a' the McGoldrick gang
A week or two at Centre Parcs, is anither holiday they like
But you should hae seen the antics, o' Cathie on a bike

At the Tuesday club in the parish hall, each week ye'll find them there
Hugh arranges a' events, for he's the person in the chair
He raises funds and organises, many a guid days outing
An' nane compares tae Hugh's clear voice, for bingo number shouting

They're baith still fit and active, a right sporting pair they are
And twice a week at carpet bools, helps keep them up to par
Ye'll no find them just sitting back, when there's something tae be done
The work they dae for ithers, is an example tae the young

The Grants have aye been awfy close, tae Cathie and tae Hugh
At a' the family weddings, we were there tae pay our due
We're proud, ye see, to hae a McGoldrick for a mother
And tho' that makes us cousins, we just call Hugh 'Our other brother'

A family reunion was arranged, in October 93
For all the McGoldrick clan, in Hugh and Sarah's family tree
That wis a night that a' were there, will always treasure dear
An' I 'm sure Hugh and Sarah that night, looked down and shed a tear

This night has been arranged, to mark a milestone in their life
Tho' he doesn't need reminding, Hugh couldn't have found a better wife
And whilst life can hae its troubles, we aye hope they're very few
And far outnumbered by the blessings, on a couple like Cathie and Hugh.

For us to say they are oor friends, is a privilege and an honour
Ye'll travel far an' never find, a better faither and a mother
So let's all charge oor glasses, wi' a toast tae Cathie and Hugh
An join wi' me tae say to them, ... May God Bless baith o' you.

Still on the subject of rhyming verse, I did similar Ruby Wedding and Golden Wedding 'poems' for one of Hugh's sisters, Cis and her husband Tam. Tam was a lovable, very loudly spoken, extrovert person, who just loved entertaining people with songs and stories.
Again it was written in the Scottish dialect:

THE RUBY WEDDING OF TAM AND CIS KERR 1995

The summer o' nineteen fifty five, wiz lang and warm and sunny
Ah remember it well - cos warm summers, we dinnae get ower mony

But theres anither reason for reminiscin', o' happenings that year
In fact, the ither reason, is the reason we're a' gaithered here

There's this quiet lad that came frae Plains, he wiz as quiet as a moose
You never heard a word frae him, ye widnae ken he wis in the hoose

Well he took this awfy fancy, to a lassie from Whinha'
Ah think they met at Airdrie Palais, well in thae days, didn't we a'

You'll no get ony prizes, for guessing who it is
The couple that I'm talkin aboot, of course it's Tam and Cis

Noo there wiznae ony Barrat homes, when Tam and Cis got wed
So they stayed wi' Cis's mammy, jist a single room and a bed

But they got a hoose in Craigneuk, and then they moved to Plains
Ah think every hoose they stayed in, they tried to fill wi' weans

Their first wee wean tae start them aff, in fifty six wiz Robbie
In fifty seven alang came Hugh, dae ye think this wis their hobby?

But they skipped a year to fifty nine, when Tom came oan the scene

In sixty one their first wee lassie, Sandy, wis a dream

Carol followed pretty soon, then Angela and Paul
Family Allowance day made Tuesday, the best weekday of all

The weans grew up as weans a' do, an' they've a' turned oot jist great
Hughie and Sarah wid be proud o' them, and so wid Dot and Kate

An' noo they're doon in Irvine, a' their weans have left the nest
But 16 happy grandchildren, meant they couldnae get a rest

So Here's tae Cis and here's tae Tam, Forty Years have come and gone
But they're still the same great couple, ... May their love go on and on.

Ten years later 2005 the following verses were added for their Golden Wedding:

So, ten mair years have come and gone, and we've gaithered here wance mair
To make their Golden Wedding, another swell affair

They now have 18 granweans, and the next generation has begun
As Tom is now a granddad, wi' the birth o' his wee son

They have special memories in the last ten years, the whole family won't forget
When 29 o' them filled 3 Florida villas, It's been the best family holiday yet

But noo they're back hame in Airdrie, an' that wis no a problem they'd to grapple
For their nice wee hoose in Johnston Street, is so handy for St Margaret's Chapel

So here's tae Cis and here's tae Tam, Fifty years have come and gone
But they're still the same great couple, …..May their love go on and on.

ON THE RAILWAY

My first job after leaving school at the end of 1953 was in a knitwear factory in Coatbridge. I only worked there for a few weeks while I was waiting to become an employee of British Railways, which had been nationalised just about five years earlier.

I had been interviewed and I think I had some kind of written test to pass before I was accepted to train as a railway booking clerk. So, early in 1954, barely 15 years old, I started my Railway career at Blairhill & Gartsherrie station in Coatbridge. My weekly wage at the knitwear factory for a 48-hour working week was £1.19.5 (pounds, shillings and pence). The top line was actually £2.3 shillings but national insurance of 3 shillings and 7 pence was deducted.

I did not pay any income tax, as at that time, you were allowed to earn £3.5 shillings of 'free pay' before income tax was deducted.

As a railway clerk I was on the 'Salaried Staff' and as such my wages was termed as salary and quoted per annum.

My starting salary was £160 PER YEAR! After deductions for national insurance my weekly take home was about £3, that was a big increase of about a £1 a week more than the factory, but still a meagre wage. After about a year I got a huge raise of £5 per annum, an increase of about 2 shillings a week. Wow!

I thoroughly enjoyed the job of being a booking clerk, selling tickets doing daily balances and daily, weekly and monthly accountancy work. Although the bookkeeping system on the Railways was single entry, as opposed the normal double entry bookkeeping in general accountancy, it certainly gave me a good grounding in all aspects of clerical and accounting work including doing pay-bills.

Prior to the war the independent Railway companies such as LNER (London & North Eastern Railway) and LMS (London, Midland, Scottish Railway) were steadily deteriorating and no money had been spent on updating rolling stock or improving and modernising railway stations.

The war years came along so nothing was done during that period and so in 1948 they were nationalised. For many years after that it was a very slow process of improvement and therefore the railway stations that I worked in were literally identical to what they must have looked like in 1900 and probably even before that.

Almost every station I worked at had no electricity and lighting was by gas mantles. Heating of the offices and waiting rooms were by coal fires.

Even when the Glasgow Electrification of trains came in 1960, I was working at the terminus of Airdrie Station and the only means of light was by gas mantles. Our trains were electric and our lighting by gas! The proper name for the station was Airdrie South and the goods station in Graham Street was Airdrie East. The points of the compass were probably the most common titles given to railway stations throughout the nation when there was more than one station in the town... North, South, East, West, Central, or Upper, Lower etc.

To get back to the gas mantles and dispel any cosy thoughts of nostalgia, consider this scenario;

I am opening the booking office door at Airdrie South on a bitterly cold January morning at 5am to get prepared for the first train departing at 5.15am. The iron keys for the door and to the safe and the parcels office are massive, each about 6 inches of cold heavy iron and you almost tear your coat pocket trying to get them out.

You are frozen, there was no heating on the bus from Calderbank to the railway station.

It's pitch black on the platform, the porter has not got round to lighting the gas mantles in the lamp-posts, he's too busy trying to get a fire started in the porters bothy.

You eventually get the booking office door open and hastily close it to stop the draught, you are inside the office and it's even darker than the platform. You fumble in your pockets to find a box of matches and strike a light. Now you can see the nearest gas mantle on the other side of the room and there doesn't seem to be any obstacles in the way, so you make your way there hoping you don't trip over anything on the floor.

The match has distinguished by this time... after slightly burning your fingers.

Before you light another match you hop your backside up on to the counter, thereby enabling you to reach the gas mantle which you light with the match. The mantle has been broken because someone yesterday used the very fragile gauze mantle to light a piece of paper to light a cigarette. That mantle is now in tatters and its effectiveness as a light is diminished by about 90%.

However, you can see sufficiently to go round and light the rest of the gas mantles in the room.

You still have your coat and scarf on and probably a pair of thick woollen gloves, you are still shivering with cold.

The next project is to get a fire going as soon as possible. You have some newspapers under some sticks and then a little coal on top. You sprinkle some paraffin from the can the porters use to fill the paraffin lamps and then you throw on a lighted match and stand well back.

This fire lighting method, although very dangerous, is the quickest way to get a warm fire going and start to thaw out the room.

The booking office window is at the opposite end of the room to the fire and it will take about two hours for any degree of heat to travel the approx. 30 feet distance.

As each customer at the window is attended to, still in your coat and scarf, you walk down the room to the fire and get another heat charge in your body. It's now almost bearable to remove your coat but certainly not your jacket *and pullover.*

After about two hours the room is near an acceptable temperature and you fill a kettle and place it on the fire for your first inviting cup of hot tea.

Very soon the chief clerk, Bertie Watson, will arrive. He sat on a high stool at a high sloping desk in the middle of the room. Directly above his head was a more elaborate gas lamp. It contained 4 mantles and was encased in a large glass globe open at the bottom, thereby allowing a lot of heat to come from the burning gas mantles and radiate down to Bertie's head.
This was a great source of heat to him and when eventually we did get electric lights in the office he complained bitterly, "Them and their bloody electric lights, I'm frozen now... Gi'e me back my gas mantles!"
He did however, get more exercise in walking to and from the fire at regular intervals.

THE HYDRAULIC LIFT AND NEAR DISASTER

There was a spell when, as a 'Summer Relief Clerk', I went to various stations to cover for clerks on holiday or sickness or even vacancies. One such assignment, which I will never forget, was at Bellgrove station in the east end of Glasgow.

The booking office was at street level and the trains, steam trains at that time, travelled underneath. When the trains came to a stop on the 'down' line, (that was on the line going in to Glasgow Queen St), the engine was directly below the booking office.

Although the engine would be stationary for only a couple of minutes, the smoke and steam emanating from it was discharged at great force and found its way up through the well worn wooden floor boards, filling the booking office with choking smoke and steam. Surprisingly I found the steam much more of an irritant than the smoke.

The first station I worked at, Blairhill & Gartsherrie, was a similar setup and the down train engines there were even more successful in filling the office with smog. The spaces between the floorboards seemed to be a bit wider there.

The incident at Bellgrove, which will never be forgotten;
The booking office, being on street level, and the platforms all down below, meant that mothers with prams had a truly difficult task in getting the prams downstairs. There weren't many folding strollers at that time and most of the prams were actually coach built prams by Churchill of Glasgow or Silver cross, weighing very heavy.

Fortunately, there was a lift from the booking hall to the platform. When I say a lift… it was an archaic contraption, a hydraulic lift operated by the power of water. Not having had physics at school, I didn't know anything about the principle behind hydraulic lifts and at that time I couldn't understand how water powered it. All I was told was to 'Pull that rope and the lift will descend, and do the same to come back up'.

It was a massive open lift constructed with very thick and heavy wood and measured approx. 8ft x 8ft. When the lift was in the booking hall, the half door gate was raised above head height and when it descended the heavy half gate would come down and rest at floor level, safeguarding anyone from falling into the empty space. This rope I had to pull, which passed through the floor and top of the lift, was situated at the opposite end from the entry. Each time a passenger came with a pram they would ask to be taken down in the lift. There was a baby boom in the 1950s, which meant that there was a steady stream of prams. The lift moved relatively slowly and I was getting a bit annoyed and disgruntled, with yo-yoing up and down in the lift. So, I hatched a plan… I'd ask the passengers with prams to stand at one side, I'd give the rope a hard tug and then run and jump out the lift before the gate came down. After all it was only about 8ft I had to cover in a quick dash.

So, I put the plan in operation… asked them to stand to one side, gave the rope a good hard pull and made a dash and jump for the open exit. Because I pulled the rope so hard the lift began to descend much more quickly. By the time I leaped to the exit we were about three feet below floor level! My knees caught the edge of the floor, the top half of my body was safely on the floor but my legs were dangling inside the empty space with the massive heavy gate descending fast to the floor.

I managed somehow to rollover, swing my legs up and over onto the safety of the floor and stare in terror as the half door crashed on to the base, where my legs were, just a fraction of a second earlier.

I lay motionless for a few moments thanking God and my Guardian Angel for sparing me from what might have been the amputation of two legs!

I can still feel the terror when I think of it, even 60 years later.

The irony of it all is that when I related the incident to the Station Master when he returned from lunch break he said "But you don't need to go in the lift at all… See that wee hole in the back wall behind the rope. You can operate it from outside the lift at the rear... Eejit!"

I did learn a serious lesson that day… the hard way... and I agreed with his assessment…an eejit!!

In the booking office at Bellgrove there was a really long table, it must have measured at least 9 or 10feet long, and I thought I was being funny with the remark, "Gosh that must have been the table they used at The Last Supper". It didn't get the response I expected from the Station Master. In fact, I was severely rebuked by him for such a blasphemous statement. I didn't try any further funny remarks with him.

When working the late shift at Bellgrove station, Tuesdays and Thursdays were the traditional evenings for lots of production workers to work overtime at the many factories in Hillington served by Hillington East and West stations.

When the hundreds of workers alighted from the trains and ran upstairs it was the clerk's job to collect the tickets and charge an 'excess fare' to those who had no ticket.

It would take a very brave man to try and stop the hordes stampeding towards you so the only answer was to hold a small basket or hat for the workers to drop their tickets in as they ran past.

When everyone had gone and the basket contents examined it revealed a few legitimate tickets, probably about 45%, but the remainder of the deposits was made up of torn woodbine cigarette packets. They were green and the same colour as legitimate tickets.

There was always a fair amount of coins, some coppers mostly 3d some 6d and even a few 1-shilling coins.

On counting all the coins, it would total around £2 to £3 and I would complete an'excess fares ticket' to that value.

On doing so, the regular porter said, "Ye cannae put a' that through... the regular clerks skin a few bob aff that, yell get them intae trouble when they get back"

"Oh?... that's tough!" I think he was just annoyed that he didn't get his cut!

After Blairhill Railway Station I was transferred to Airdrie South Railway Station.

Note: I refer to them as 'railway stations', not 'train stations', which seems to be the common practice now. For well over 100 years they were called 'railway stations' and it irritates me intensely to hear them referred to as 'train stations'. I think most railway employees of my generation would agree with me. Maybe I'm just becoming a grumpy old man! After all, we have always referred to 'bus stations' so why not 'train stations'.

Whilst I worked at Blairhill station there were still a few trains to Edinburgh Waverley via Bathgate but this service was discontinued and the passenger line terminated at Airdrie by the time I went to work there.

In the 50s and early 60s parcels represented a substantial proportion of railway business.

Being the terminus, Airdrie served a number of villages in the surrounding area; Calderbank, Chapelhall, Plains, Caldercruix, Slamannan, Glenmavis and Longriggend to mention a few.

It was still steam trains then and almost every train arriving at Airdrie had a number of parcels in the guards van.

I say 'parcels' but every item was a referred to as a parcel, boxes, cartons, bicycles, toys and suitcases. There were also boxes of fresh fish from Aberdeen, dripping water from the thawing ice and smelling strongly. They arrived about 3pm or 4pm each day and were collected by a well known Airdrie worthy named Harry Roy, more about Harry in another part of this book.

Other sample parcels included tools, motor parts, hired suits for Dan-

skins tailor shop in Graham Street, even tailor's dummies, is it politically correct now to say that…or should it be mannequins?
Occasionally we would receive coffins, empty of course. Livestock
was very common too, racing pigeons especially, and the occasional
dog which of course had to be on a collar and leash.
I distinctly remember one of the old porters running along the up platform chasing a small terrier dog, shouting… "Catch that dog… it's a
parcel!"

Frightening Dreams

Friday nights were 'racing pigeon' nights and there were dozens of
pigeon baskets all over the platform. The local Pigeon Society had to
register all pigeons participating in the race and had a great deal of
documentation to do.
The Waiting Room on the Up platform, no longer used by passengers
since the Edinburgh service ended, was used as the Parcels Office. It
was the booking clerk's duty to regularly record all details of every
parcel received on the delivery sheets, in preparation for the 'carters'
to effect their daily deliveries within the town and the surrounding
areas.
At regular intervals, after a Glasgow train would depart, I would cross
the railway line to the parcels office. I should always have obeyed the
'Cross the Railway Line By The Footbridge Only' sign but I rarely
did so. Being young and fit… and stupid! I would jump down on to
the track and dart across the lines and in one leap jump up on to the
other platform.
I would however check that the Station Master was not in sight!
This action must have preyed on my subconscious. For many years, I
would have this recurring dream;

*I jump down on to the line even though there is a train approaching on the
up line. I get to the point where I am about to leap up onto the platform
when my legs and my whole body become paralysed! I am unable to move*

an inch; the train is almost upon me. Then I awaken in a terrible sweat, my heart thumping at a colossal rate.

It was all so totally realistic! This dream continued regularly for a few years, even after I had left that occupation.
However, a similar recurring dream replaced this but instead of an approaching train, this time I was driving a car!

The car was in reverse, always in reverse, and travelling at speed, the brakes were ineffective! I had to frantically attempt to steer this speeding car and it was an impossible situation.
Again, I'd wake up in a sweat and heart thumping!

Perhaps some dream analyst could interpret the meaning of my terrifying dreams. I think it is a case of me not being in control and/or a lack of security. Thankfully I have only rarely experienced such dreams in my later years and certainly not since I retired.
When I did work with British Railways I was always aware of the smell of a railway station. No matter what station I visited they all had the same smell, the booking offices, waiting rooms, porter's bothies, signal boxes... all of them seemed to have the same odour.
It was not a bad smell, not at all, it was... well... distinctive. Railway employees seemed to have this odour impregnated in their clothes, if you were on a bus or tram you could detect that a railwayman was on board when you got that railway sniff.
Some 30 years later when I was a Sub Postmaster at a busy sub office in Ayr, I was serving at the counter and I got that distinctive 'sniff'. I asked the man if he worked on the Railway and I would have been disappointed had he answered in the negative, but my nose didn't let me down, he was a railwayman.

I was never one for rising too early in the morning and when I was on an early shift I would only give myself a calculated number of minutes from when I arose, to wash, tea and toast and out the door.
This allowed me to stay in bed as long as possible. In the summer

months, I would often cycle from Calderbank to catch the first train from Airdrie at about 6am. This was when it was still steam trains.

The guard on the train would know me and on the occasions when I cut things too fine, I would reach the platform just as the train began to pull away. Steam trains started very slowly thankfully. I would shout to the guard and chase the slow moving train until I past the guards van. I would swing off the bike, the guard would grab it and take it into the guards van and I would run alongside and grab the rail and hop on into the van.

That was a dangerous and stupid thing to do and of course against Railway Bye Laws. All because I wanted a couple of minutes more in my bed! Well when you are young you think you are invincible. The truth is I was a stupid eejit again but I got away with it without accident.

My Guardian Angel often had to work overtime!

WEE HARRY ROY

Every town, and probably every village in Scotland, had what was commonly called their 'local worthies' or 'characters' and Airdrie, in my young days, was no exception.

These were characters that everyone in the town knew, even if they had never spoken to them, because of their appearance, habits, notoriety, drunkenness, achievements or anything else that made them stand out from the crowd.

Even as late as the 1940s and 50s, most people lived, worked and socialised within their own town or village and did not travel too far distant for any reason. Except perhaps the occasional day trip to the Ayrshire coast or a 'mystery tour' bus run, where you didn't even know where you were going. We often wondered if even the bus driver knew.

A journey on the old shoogly trams to Glasgow was considered a 'day out' and my favourite part of the trams was the upstairs compartment at the front. This was the shoogliest part of the tram on the older 'Standard' trams before the 'Coronation' model was introduced.

It is little wonder then that most people knew, or knew of, any character in the town. Everyone knew their neighbours then, aye and helped them when the need arose.

Often these characters could be described as 'a lovable rogue' but some were known for more sinister reasons like drunkenness, fighting, exhibitionism and worse.

As a young boy walking to and from school in Hallcraig Street in Airdrie, I would pass the small gents public toilet situated at the right hand side of Anderson Street, just before the corner with Bank Street. Very often there was a man who stood there just inside the small smelly toilet and he scared me no end! He was dirty, smelly, unshaven and always had a cigarette sticking out his mouth. He stood on one leg and a crutch. His other twisted leg, the left one, only reached about nine inches from the ground and his left arm seemed to be twisted and paralysed.

As you squeezed past him he mumbled, "have ye got a fag". I ignored him but then the twisted left hand struck out at you, so it wasn't paralysed.

He didn't hit you, it was just to frighten you. Well he succeeded with me. Thereafter, if he was there I would rather pee my trousers than try to squeeze past him or go to the other smelly toilet down the steps into Market Street, straight across from the town clock in Bank Street. They say you never forget a smell, well that's for sure the way both these toilets stank, you had to be really desperate to use either of those two.

My old granny, although of Irish descent, used a great many old Scots phrases. One of them was when describing a person whom today we call a 'born again Christian', she would say "He's foun' the Lord". Well there was a certain character in Airdrie who led a life of drunkenness and all that goes with that until he 'Found the Lord'.

He then could be seen with, what we disrespectfully referred to as 'The Hallelujahs', a gathering of a few people in a circle on Sunday afternoons and evenings. Listening to one of them preaching, trying to save souls and imploring everyone to turn to God. Interspersing the bible readings and preaching with the singing of hymns.

Now, this reformed person I am referring to was a big strong rough looking man and for those who knew his past he really looked out of place. However when the group started singing the hymns this man really came into his own, especially when he belted out 'How Great Thou Art'.

He had a voice that would not have been out of place in a concert hall and many locals would stop and be entertained listening to his renditions. Whether he succeeded in conversions of the souls is another matter.

These religious circles on Sundays were common in every town. In Airdrie they gathered at the foot of Hallcraig Street just opposite what was the Rialto picture house. If my memory serves me, there was an extra tall street lamp in the middle of the road where Hallcraig Street and Mill Street met South Bridge Street and Bank Street and that's where they preached and sang hymns.

I also remember similar preachers coming round the tenement back doors, doing their preaching and singing. Those ones usually had some musical instruments and they too would sit or stand in a circle.

The one character who really stands out in my memory was truly a 'lovable rogue'. Everybody in Airdrie knew him and loved him. He was very small in stature but very big in popularity. He was Harry Roy.

At a height of only about 5ft. 3 or 4 inches, everyone prefixed his name with the word 'wee' and Wee Harry Roy was most often seen wheeling his barrow around the town.

His old flat wooden wheelbarrow was fairly long and had no sides, two back legs, one front wheel and a wooden front to stop things falling off when lifted.

A photo of Harry is reproduced in the centre section of the book, courtesy of the Airdrie & Coatbridge Advertiser. This photo appeared in 1988 when the newspaper was publishing a regular feature, 'All Our Yesterdays'.

It stated there that the photograph was taken about 30 years earlier, which would make it about 1958 and that certainly was how I remember Harry and his barrow.

A barrow of this style was suitable therefore for carting pieces of furniture and other items that balanced in the middle of the barrow. It was not uncommon to see Harry wheeling a sideboard or small wardrobe or a fireside couch chair. It was rumoured that Harry did 'flittings' with his barrow.

Because of it's style and only having a front wheel, he was taking a fair percentage of the weight when transporting items, and pushing uphill was very heavy work, especially for a wee man like Harry so he would often stop for a rest and was keen to have a word or two with anyone passing.

Harry always had a cute answer for those who thought they were being smart with him. He was never short of a witty response that was totally appropriate.

Harry wore a long coat almost down to his ankles but it never seemed to be buttoned. In warmer weather it would be just a jacket and waistcoat and again the jacket was never buttoned. Whether it was the coat or the jacket, they seemed to hang loose, almost falling off his shoulders. No matter what the weather was like he always wore a bunnet, as did most working class men in the 1940s.

Another well-known man in Airdrie, was the preacher at the Mission Hall in High Street, diagonally opposite our house. His name was Mr Johnston and we always referred to him as 'the Town Missioner'. Mr Johnston was the very antithesis of Harry, he was very tall, probably about 6ft.4 inches, always perfectly dressed in a long black coat and a bowler hat. Harry had quite a squeaky voice and of course spoke in a guid Scottish tongue but Mr Johnston was very refined and polite.

I was passing both these characters in the Wellwynd. The Wellwynd ran from the West Parish church at the bottom, uphill to High Street at the top. It was a fairly steep sloping street or brae to use a good Scottish term, and when the snow arrived in winter it was our favourite sledging hill. I also remember clinging on to the back of lorries, which could only travel very slowly up the hill when fully loaded. That was a foolish and dangerous thing to do but we never thought of it as such at the time.

Anyway, to get back to their meeting halfway up the street. Harry had stopped for a rest, flicked his bunnet to the back of his head and sat on the edge of the barrow, looking a wee bit exhausted.

Mr Johnston looked at him and surmising that it was heavy work for Harry, tried to give him some encouragement in saying to him "Aye Harry, where there's a will, there's a way".

Harry lifted his eyes to the Town Missioner, paused momentarily, then responded "Aye, and where there's a hill there's a brae". He was never stuck for an answer.

I personally had a good relationship with Harry. You see one of the 'contracts' that Harry had with his barrow was to go to Airdrie South railway station (I refuse to call it train station) every day around 3pm or 3.30pm to collect a number of boxes of fish which were sent daily from Aberdeen.

It was steam trains in those days and the boxes came off the Aberdeen train at Glasgow Queen St. and then put on a train to Airdrie.

Harry loaded them onto his barrow and then wheeled them to various fish and chip shops in the town. Luchinie's, in Aitchieson Street, Lamarra's, in East High Street, Ben Bianchi's in South Bridge Street (or was it called Zambonini's then?) and a few other chip shops.

Harry would often lift a box of fish onto his head, still wearing his bunnet, to carry them into the shops. Now these boxes, which measured about 18inches by 20 inches and about 8inches deep, had the haddock or whiting fish packed in ice. So by the time they got from Aberdeen to Airdrie they were dripping of melted ice. Can you imagine how Harry's bunnet smelled?

I soon found out that Harry was keen to get some young boys like me to help him wheel his barrow of fish round the town. Our payment was a poke of chips and sometimes with a bit of fish, which Harry would get free gratis from chip shops.

Chips was my favourite meal, hence my willingness to be one of Harry's boys.

There was one day a week when all the chip shops in the town were closed. I think it was a Tuesday and as I spent most of my pocket money on a 2d poke of chips, I did not like Tuesdays.

Airdrie's Employment Exchange commonly referred to as 'The Broo' was situated in Anderson Street opposite the General Post Office. Unemployed people had to 'sign on the Broo' every week to get their unemployment benefit. I think the term 'Broo' was a Scottish pronunciation of the word bureau and perhaps it was previously called the 'Employment Bureau'.

A couple of stories went around about Harry and his escapades in 'The Broo'.

Now remember, it was only unemployed men that signed on each week.

There was normally a queue of people lining up to sign whatever form was required to be signed but Harry would come in and go to the front of the queue saying "Here let me in, Ah've ma work to get tae, Ah'm gonnae be late".

Well everybody knew he had the fish to deliver and they wanted their fish suppers so…

On another occasion in 'the Broo', Harry signed his name on the form and slid it back to the clerk. He didn't lean very heavily with the pen on the paper and so his signature was not very legible.

The clerk pushed the form back to Harry and said "Here Harry, I can't read yer name, it's too feint, Put yer weight on it".

Harry obliged and wrote on the form "8stone 4lbs."

Then there was the time when Harry got to the front of the queue and the clerk had been a wee bit abrupt with the client in front of Harry and was a bit flustered.

He slid the form across the desk too strongly and it flew down onto the floor. The bold Harry got down on his knees and signed the form where it lay on the floor and left it there. He got up, turned around and said "Cheerio son" as he left the building.

A few years after my service as one of Harry's barrow boys, I was working as a railway booking clerk at Airdrie station. Harry was still running his fish transporting business and I was on duty when the steam train that would normally bring in the boxes of fish arrived. However, there was no fish on board.

An irate Harry came over to the booking office and demanded that I find out what happened to his fish boxes. "If they're no on the next train fae Queen Street they'll be nae use to the Tallies, so let me speak to Queen Street".

Railway stations at that time had an internal phone communication system. It was normally an old- fashioned wooden phone box with a speaker part and was affixed to the wall. On the side of the box there was a hook to hold the hearing piece of the phone.

To call any station on the line or any signal box, each had a call code. For example, it could be two bells then one bell then two more. You soon got to know when someone was trying to contact you. There was no connection on this system to Queen Street parcels office but in an attempt to appease Harry I rang the signal box at the end of the platform at Airdrie station.

"Is that Queen Street Parcels" I said "Ah've got Harry Roy here complaining about no fish being on that train that's just arrived at Airdrie, he wants to speak to you"

The signalman caught on to what I was doing and played along. I gave the hearing piece to Harry and he had to stand on his tiptoes to get his mouth near the speaking piece.

"Where's ma fish? It shoulda been oan that last train, where is it?"

I don't know what the signalman said to him but it obviously didn't go down well with Harry.

"Look, ah'll pull you through this fuckin phone if you don't get ma fish on the next train, ya eejit" The signalman, it appeared, just hung up the phone leaving Harry even more irate.

"That shite's ran away, well he better get ma fish or there'll be nae fish suppers the night in Airdrie".

I think Harry was well aware of what we were doing and played along, he in fact was just humouring us instead of us humouring him.

It is just dawning on me now that the old wall fixed phones would have been the norm in the early days of telephones and when you hung up the hearing piece it cut off the line. So that's probably how the saying 'he hung up on me' came about.

I cannot recall clearly, but this occasion of the fish coming in very late, was probably one where the booking office had to dispose of any perishable goods under the 'Salvage' rule. In other words if the consignee refused the consignment for any legitimate reason, in this case it certainly was legitimate, we had to attempt to sell the goods at whatever price we could get, thereby salvaging something to offset the compensation claim which would obviously follow.

The staff at the station, plus all the friends and neighbours they could contact, were very happy to pay about 6d. for a few pounds of filleted haddock and whiting. It provided good and very cheap meals for the family for a day or two... 'It's an ill wind, and all that'.

CONSCRIPTED:
ARMY NATIONAL SERVICE

Conscription for all men into military service was introduced in 1939 at the outbreak of the Second World War by The National Service (Armed Forces) Act. After the war, National Service as peacetime conscription was formulated by The National Service Act 1948. Conscription continued for all men born before 1st October 1939 so that meant I was obliged to serve Queen and Country. Two of my older brothers, who were 6 years and 8 years my senior, did their National Service long before I was due to be called up at age 18. My oldest brother John was a time served tradesman, a fitter, and as such his service was deferred until his apprenticeship was completed. He, therefore, was not called up to serve with The Royal Artillery until he was 21. Unfortunately for him he was posted to an active zone in Egypt. In 1952, Egyptian Army officers, led by Neguib and Colonel Nasser, started a revolution to overthrow King Faruk and end the monarchy and later work towards ending the British occupation of Egypt and control of the Suez Canal.

John was amongst those sent to the Suez Canal zone and they were living in tents in Fayid alongside the Suez Canal. Revolutionary snipers were constantly attacking them. In the conflict about 47 British soldiers were killed, thankfully John returned home safely. Apart from serving in Egypt, John was also stationed, again billeted in tents, in Cyprus, which was, at that time, still under British rule. At least he came home with a good tan.

He was 'demobbed', or to use the proper word, demobilized, just before I left school in 1953. I can still clearly picture in my mind the day he arrived home. I was off school with a cold or flu, no one else was at home when John arrived carrying his kit bag. None of us knew he was due to arrive home and in those days we did not have telephones in the house. Perhaps he sent a letter telling us to expect him but he arrived before the letter. We both hugged one another and, unashamedly, cried with joy. I hadn't seen him for about two years. Even as I write this, tears come to my eyes once again.

Nasser eventually took command in Egypt and in 1956 he seized control of the Suez Canal. This was known as the 'Suez Crisis'.

Britain, France and Israel, in response, invaded Egypt in late 1956 to regain Western control of the Canal and remove President Nasser from power.

Now, at this time, late 1956, I reached my 18th birthday and therefore was liable for call up to National Service. This invasion by the British Army made me very nervous. No way was I wishing to follow my brother John's experience of fighting the Egyptians.

Whilst I was basically a pacifist, or maybe just a devout coward, I would not have had the guts to be a conscientious objector. No, that takes great courage.

As it turned out, the Prime Minister, Anthony Eden, did not get support from the USA for the Suez invasion and very soon ordered an end to the Suez operation and resigned as Prime minister.

Phew, that was close and very scary but there was still unrest in Cyprus in 1958. I could have been posted to that island and confront General Grivas or a more reasonable Archbishop Makarios who wanted an independent Cyprus through peaceful means. My brother Jim was not called up for National Service due to health reasons but my other brother, Joe, did have to do his duty. In actual fact he signed on for the extra year, I think, to get into the Royal Air Force rather than the Army. After initial training he was stationed in Oldenberg in Germany.

Although I was 18 yrs. old in November 1956, I didn't receive communication from the War Office about my National Service until well into 1957. Now I thought I would prefer to serve my Queen in the Royal Air Force, 'the Brylcreem Boys', as I thought it would be a bit more cushy, and I liked the uniform better.

However, they were only occasionally taking conscripts into the RAF and the choice was not available to me, so I thought I would do as my brother Joe had done and sign on for three years. After all you got paid much more and it looked an easy option.

I went through the process and filled in all the required forms, had my medical and in due course received instructions to report to RAF Cardington where all new entrants to the RAF commenced their service.

By this time in 1957, my brother Joe was also demobbed from the RAF and when he saw that I was intent on joining for three years he asked to see my papers.

I obediently handed them to him and to my amazement he systematically tore all the papers into shreds. I was gobsmacked, as well as being a bit apprehensive.

"Whit the hell are ye doing", I said.

"You're not going in for three years", was his stern response.

"Well you done three years, did ye not".

"Aye, and that's why you're not, two years is long enough", and so, it came to pass that I was not going to Cardington... or the RAF.

Having not turned up at the RAF, I just waited and waited to see what would happen. Maybe they'll just forget about me or have lost my papers somewhere, or some careless clerk doesn't follow through with the process. I lived in hope.

Around that time, I was working as a Railway booking clerk and had made good friends with a colleague, Johnny Trower. Johnny and I seriously discussed the prospect of taking advantage of the '£10 Assisted Passage Scheme' to emigrate to Australia.

A six-week luxury cruise to Sunny Australia for just £10 and the opportunity of a new lifestyle did appeal to me. My friend Johnny, did in fact go through with this and settled in Adelaide. We have kept in communication and he has visited us on a few occasions over the years.

I, however, got my call-up papers. I still have that enlistment notice, I was ordered to report to the Royal Army Pay Corps training centre at Devizes in Wiltshire on Thursday 6th February 1958.

That date, 6th of February 1958, is one that I will never forget, not just because it was the day I joined the Army, but for another reason. On that day, the Manchester United football team, the famous 'Busby Babes', were flying from Munich Airport when the plane crashed on it's third attempt to take off from a slush covered runway.

In that air crash 23 people died and it became known as 'The Munich Air Disaster'.

There is also another, very personal reason, that 6th of February is such an important date for me. Eight years later, on 6th February 1966, our first daughter, Maureen, was born.

Over the years I have teased her about the three 'disasters' of the 6th of February and the biggest disaster of them all… the birth of Mo.

In my life there have been a few incredible coincidences. One of them was travelling by train to arrive at Devizes in Wiltshire for my Army service.

National Service intakes were every two weeks and always on a Thursday. As most Army and RAF barracks were in England and it was railway travel warrants that were supplied to the conscripts, trains from Glasgow Central, every second Wednesday evening, were pretty much filled with raw recruits travelling to various parts of the country. I joined the train at Motherwell station and I would guess the train comprised of about eight carriages, so you can imagine several hundred passengers would be on board the train.

When I boarded at Motherwell and walked along the corridor looking for a suitable apartment, I settled on one which looked as though there were more lads in the same situation that I was in…. they were raw recruits.

That was the case and there were about eight of us in the compartment. We didn't sleep much, not least by the smell of sweaty feet, but we played cards and talked and laughed and joked most of night.

It turned out that there were actually two others in that compartment who were actually going to Devizes and the Pay Corps! That in itself, is quite a coincidence, but it doesn't end there.

The next day, after we were all kitted out and allocated our billet (sixteen beds in one large wooden hut), we were given our army numbers.

My army number, which no soldier ever forgets, was 23452120.

The fellow I was sat next to on the train was given the army number next to mine. I cannot remember now whether it was 2345 2121 or 2119.

Of the hundreds on the train the previous night I sit next to him… incredible.

On the first day we arrived at Devizes railway station, we were met by the training sergeants and corporals who yelled out their orders interspersed with every swear word you could imagine.

This, of course, was just to instil fear in you and confirm that all the stories you had heard about Army training were true.

We soon found out that when you were all told to do something or go somewhere, it was to be at the double. If you were last, there would be punishment, so you soon knew the routine but sadly it was usually the same boys that came last in everything. I was pretty active and fast so I never came last, there were other circumstances though, where they caught me out and I got a little share of the punishments, but not very often.

On the first day, we were taken to the Quartermaster's stores to be kitted out.

"You will be issued here with a full set of equipment and at the end you will sign form AF*** (whatever the number was) to confirm that you have received all that you should", the Sergeant bawled out.

"And you'll move along the counter quickly".

This was the nearest thing to a conveyor belt operation. The first item you were given was a kit bag as all the supplies you were issued with were to be put in the kit bag. You then moved along the long counter with QM staff throwing the supplies to you, shouting…

"Stockings, woollen, 4 pairs",
"Khaki uniform, trousers and BD jacket",
"Denim uniform, trousers and BD jacket",
"Underpants, cotton, Khaki, 2 pairs… Belt Khaki, one", and so on…
until all your kit had been supplied. When it came to your boots they
asked what size and threw them at you, no trial fit. I think I asked for
size 7 but as it turned out, with the thick grey woollen socks, a size 7
was too small.

Later, when I complained that they were too wee they said, "you
signed for them, you asked for that size, you're stuck with them"

We were not issued with shoes so constant wearing of boots that were
too small resulted in me suffering from ingrown toenails, which later
proved to be a good skive for me. I will elaborate on that later.

After we were issued with all our kit and had taken it to our billet, we
were then all given the traditional, new recruit, Army haircut… an
almost bald back and sides, with less than half an inch of hair on top.
In 1958, the hairstyle for young men was definitely not short hair. My
preferred hairstyle was the 'Tony Curtis'.

The haircut was also a conveyor type operation and only took about
3 minutes per man.

How this haircut changed one's appearance was truly remarkable. So
much so, that one of the lads with whom I had spent the previous
night on the train, actually did not recognize me, nor I him, when we
first met after the 'baldy'.

Incidentally, we had to pay sixpence for that haircut which was deducted from your first week's pay.

Talking about pay, the first 18 months of service we only got paid, I
think, £1.4.6d per week. From that I sent seven shillings a week home
to my mother (by means of a payment book paid at the post office),
so in actual fact 17 shillings and 6 pence was my lot every week…
not even £1.

To put things into perspective, a pint of beer in the pub would cost
about one shilling, a pack of 10 cigarettes about 1/6d. Cinema admis-
sion would be about the same as pack of cigs and dancing at the local
Palais about two shillings.

So, for most of my Army days stationed in Newcastle–upon-Tyne, when we got paid on a Thursday we went out that night, two or three pints in the pub, a packet of fags and then went to the dancing and got a fish supper on the walk home. That would total about ten shillings for the night out... ten bob, half a £1.

That left very little for the remaining 6 days. On many occasions, three or four of us would be sharing a cigarette between us, take a drag and pass it on! On most nights therefore we could buy a tea and pack of crisps in the NAAFI (Navy, Army & Air Force Institution), a sort of café/canteen, which the organisation provided at all Service barracks.

After the 3 months initial training at the Royal Army Pay Corps barracks in Devizes, Wiltshire, I was stationed at Fenham Barracks in Newcastle which was the home of the Northumberland Fusiliers but they were in new premises and we occupied the their old antiquated buildings.

One of the spare rooms on the ground floor was equipped with table tennis and a wireless and that was just about the only leisure activity that was provided for us.

Try playing table tennis on knot ridden wooden floors wearing tackety boots, sliding everywhere, while listening to Pat Boone singing 'April Love' or 'Love Letters in the Sand' on the radio. Which reminds me, it was on this radio one night in February 1959 when the sad news of Buddy Holly's death in an air crash was announced.

There was only four of us who were posted to Newcastle after training and on the first '48 hour pass', that means a weekend when soldiers could go home, I did not do so. I hadn't enough money to get there for the weekend so on the Saturday night I went to one of the cinemas in central Newcastle, on my own.

This was the time of the 'Teddy Boy' gangs and often they were out looking for trouble and causing a disturbance.

Walking home from the cinema I could see ahead and coming towards me were about 7 or 8 'Teddy Boys'. As I may have mentioned before, I am a devout coward and prefer to avoid confrontation, more especially when the odds are so much not in my favour.

I gave them a wide berth, so wide I stepped onto the road, and held my breath when passing them. After we were about 20 yards apart, I thought that's fine they're not going to bother with me when suddenly a Newcastle Brown ale empty bottle smashed on the pavement just in front of me.

Turning round whilst I simultaneously got into top gear I could see what I feared. They were coming for me! Well I had just finished my 3 months army training and was quite fit, I was always a very fast runner over the 100 yards, so none of them had a hope of catching me. I ran very much more than 100 yards before I looked back and they were not in sight.

Newcastle had a reputation of being a wee bit rough at times but I must admit that there was only one other occasion when I was 'jumped on'.

A few of us had been to a local dance hall in the north of Newcastle, it was cheaper to get in there than the fashionable 'Majestic' in the centre of town.

I asked one of the girls I had danced a couple of times if I could walk her home and she was very agreeable. The homes in the area where she lived resembled the back-to-back lanes you see in the early days of TV's Coronation Street.

We had just turned off the main road into what I believed was her street, about 30 yards down the street someone jumped on my back. It turned out it was the girl's boy friend, or maybe ex boy friend.

There were three of them however. Again, the odds were not in my favour but thankfully there were no real blows struck. They indicated that it would be wise of me to just depart, intact... or suffer any consequences.

My devout cowardice overcame me again and I took them up on their kind offer and said goodnight to the girl who did not seem too perturbed about the incident.

We seemed to be constantly hungry and rarely had any money to buy any food so after the evening dinner in the canteen you just starved till breakfast in the morning.

A wee confession here, there was a couple of occasions, when in a state of malnutrition, a few of us broke into the cookhouse, found some bread, fried a few eggs and enjoyed a late evening meal.

A fair percentage of the soldiers at our barracks in Newcastle were Scottish, the Army were being very considerate here in stationing us quite near home.

When we had a '48 hour pass' allowing us to go home at the weekend we usually came back with Scottish £1 notes. They differed from the Bank of England notes, were different in colour and more the size of the English £5 note.

Although we were billeted in Fenham Barracks, the offices where we worked were a few miles north in Ponteland and there was a wee shop opposite which sold newspapers, fags, crisps, lemonades etc. so many of the soldiers frequented this shop.

The owner of the shop, a Mrs McKenzie, (see that, I still remember her name), contacted the Adjutant complaining that one of the soldiers gave her a Scottish pound note, and she mistakenly gave him change of a fiver. The Adjutant gathered us all on pay day and related the story asking that the guilty person make good the £4 "which he stole!"

The soldier concerned, George, was a very popular likeable rogue, not a bad lad at all, but £4 was a lot of money when you are so poorly paid and the temptation was too much for him.

However, George did go to the shop a day or so later with the £4.

"Mrs McKenzie, the fellow who got this is very sorry for not telling you at the time but he is too ashamed and he asked me if I would take this £4 back for him, he's really very sorry"

Mrs Mac was only too happy to get her 'stolen' £4 returned, she gave George a bar of chocolate for his bother. He still felt guilty at eating the chocolate… but it didn't make him sick.

I was in the Royal Army Pay Corps, (R.A.P.C.) stationed in Newcastle and our duties were to maintain the pay records of all the Royal Army Service Corps, Regular and National Service soldiers serving in the UK and Germany.

Maintaining their pay records meant that for every soldier there was a page in the account books which recorded everything to do with pay and any event which affected their level of pay. If they got married, they got a marriage allowance added. If they were stationed overseas, that was an overseas allowance. Some would have payment books issued to their mother or wife. If they were imprisoned, payments were stopped. Anything that affected their rate of pay was controlled and recorded by us at Newcastle, in total there were possibly the pay accounts of about 6000 personnel.

There were six account departments with 6 account clerks in each section, which meant if they were divided equally each clerk would deal with about 160 or 170 soldiers. However, the book of accounts I was allotted contained over 300 soldiers and I remember I looked after all soldiers with surnames beginning with the letter 'R' and a number beginning with 'S'.

Rees, Reid, Read, Rede, Reed, Rhys, Richards, Robertson, Russell… so many of them came from Wales.

So in effect, I was handling about twice as many as the average clerk, though in doing so, I gained great experience of any events that affected the soldier's pay.

This stood me in good stead when the time for the annual 'Trade Tests' came up after about six months service. The result of your test graded you as B2, B3 or B4. I achieved 98% in the test and the Commanding Officer, a Colonel, sent for me.

He was so proud that one of his soldiers actually got the highest mark in Trade Tests, in the whole of Eastern Command of all Army personnel, in all regiments.

He told me that I would be transferred to the 'Office Inspection Team', the compliment of which should have consisted of a Captain, a Staff Sergeant and a Sergeant. In effect, it was a small team of auditors.

"We will promote you to Lance Corporal initially and further promotion will follow".

Well the *will follow* aspect never did materialise but the appointment to this small team which actually only consisted of myself, a Sergeant and another Lance Corporal, was a welcome move.

As inspection auditors, we could randomly go into any accounts section and choose an accounts book and search for errors, overpayments, fraudulent payment books etc. I actually uncovered a number of instances where payment books were still being cashed at post offices even though the soldiers had left the service.

The main thing that pleased me was that so long as I had a wee piece of notepaper with a name and Army number on it I could wander about any section or department in the guise that I was 'auditing'. This was the 'skive' that suited me to a T.

I mentioned earlier about another 'skive' due to my ingrown toenails, the result of having to wear boots that were too small for me.

Each morning we would muster on the parade ground at the barracks and be marched to the lorries to be transported to the offices.

If you were reporting sick, which I did very often due to my ingrown toenails, you did not join the muster parade and just hung around the barrack room until it was time to attend the doctor.

There was also a 'duty sergeant' who would occasionally walk around all the barrack rooms to ensure there was no one there who should have been on the lorries. I did not want to be confronted by him and perhaps given some undesirable duties until the doc's appointment.

I could hear his heavy boot footsteps on the wooden floor and quickly opened the door of the narrow metal wardrobe, which each soldier had beside his bed. I would squeeze in there beside my great coat, pull the door closed and wait until the sound of footsteps indicated that he had completed the inspection of the room and moved on.

This happened on two occasions and thankfully I was not discovered. It would have made sense of course if they just supplied me with a bigger size of boots, or more preferably a pair of shoes, but that was a no-no.

Eventually, I was sent to the Army Hospital at Catterick to have my toenails removed but they didn't remove the nail roots so the nails did eventually grow back in.

Before this happened, there was the annual rifle firing marksman tests at a shooting range somewhere out in the country.

We were, for some reason, taken there in coaches rather than the usual lorries. I was in the first batch of soldiers being assessed and fired the regulation number of bullets at the large targets.

In a trench in front of the targets was the 'butt markers' who would indicate where the bullets landed. Now to my surprise, although I knew I had good eyesight (I was the 'eagle eye' in the Scouts), I got top marks and was awarded a Marksman Badge, which was sewn on to the bottom of the arm of my uniform. If I'm honest I think the butt marker at my target just used a pencil to push through the canvas target to look like a bullet hit.

Anyway, after our platoon had been tested, we were just hanging about and that's just not allowed in the Army.

A young National Service officer, a sub lieutenant, decided that he would take us on a 90-minute march into the countryside. My toenails were playing up and I started limping and the officer noticed that. "What's wrong with you soldier".

"I have ingrown toenails sir, I have been attending the medical dept.".

"Right, dismiss and stay in the bus until we return". ... Now that worked out well, did it not?

Less than 30 minutes after they left on their march, the heavens opened and torrential rain fell for the next 40 minutes. I was comfortable and dry in the bus. Those on the firing range and in the butt trenches and those on the march got soaked through to the skin. I should have felt guilty I suppose but I didn't. When anyone outside came anywhere near the bus I ducked down out of sight.

When the marchers eventually returned to the bus, they were, understandably, pretty jealous.

Yes, these were some of the skives I took advantage of but in civilian life I was by no means a skiver, in fact I was the complete opposite, hard working and industrious. So why was I like that in the Army?

Well, we were National Servicemen, not willing recruits and by the late 1950s conscription was really not necessary, so in my mind, this was a complete waste of time and resources.

I was, and I suppose I still am, a natural rebel against the establishment, a supporter of the underdog, a socialist, a believer in equality and justice, and a pacifist (or at least anti-war). So, being compelled to serve Her Majesty for two years (I am also anti-monarchist), this went against the grain.

Now in saying all that, whilst I would not have volunteered for the Army, I do not regret having completed National Service, in fact I am glad I did have this experience. I'm sure, in some ways, it contributed to my character building. It certainly taught me discipline, obeying orders without question (that wrangled me a bit), camaraderie, teamwork, endurance, loyalty, flexibility and adaptability and working under pressure.

These qualities I carried into civilian life and I recall the written statement of my Commanding Officer on my 'Certificate of National Service', a small booklet issued to a soldier on his discharge. Colonel Burdet wrote the following:

"Has done a very good job of work during his national Service. A very capable and competent clerk who is neat and accurate in his work. Works without supervision and can be relied upon to produce good results. Will undoubtedly do well in civilian life. Uses his intelligence and initiative in his work. A loyal, willing and hard working man who is reliable and trustworthy. A pleasant disposition, good manners, smart appearance, and always well turned out. A good type of young man."

Now how the hell could he write that about me?... I only spoke to him once in all the time I was there.

I searched out this certificate from a collection of old stuff in a suitcase up in the loft and was a wee bit surprised that I still had it after almost 60 years.

The two lines that always stood out in my mind were 'A good type of young man' and 'Will undoubtedly do well in civilian life'. Well I am not going to disagree with those sentiments and I suppose the old Colonel got it just about right.

A couple of other items from my Army days were stored beside this certificate. One was my 'Days to Do' chart. All the National Servicemen longed for, and greatly anticipated, demob day and most of us created a chart for the last 100 days of service.

It would be displayed at their work desk and each day they would ceremoniously strike off another day, bragging to the others who joined after them that they still had a long time to do.

" Days to do, ...very few, ... less than you... (I wont relate the last words, they're a bit indecent).

Although we were very poorly paid, each of us set up a savings fund in the final six months, putting a regular amount away each pay day to go towards the 'Demob Party'.

All the savings, of course, would be spent in the chosen pub on our final night in the Army.

There were three others being demobbed along with me and we decided to have our farewell night together with our selected friends. We chose a pub in the 'Bigg Market' in the centre of Newcastle.

We were allocated an upstairs room for our private function and there was some serious drinking until closing time, which would be about 10pm. Understandably, I cannot recall too much of that night but to give testament to the quantity of alcohol consumed, one member of the party fell down the stairs and ended up in the Victoria Infirmary and two others were escorted to cells in Newcastle Police station.

I don't know what misdemeanours they were guilty of, I could guess of course, but anyway they deserved our support and loyalty.

A few of us, who were still capable of walking, made our way to the police station in an attempt to persuade the boys in blue that our comrades should be allowed to go home with rest of us. We were unable to convince the lawmen and in fact we were given a two-minute ultimatum to disperse or a promise to be joining our two friends inside. Common sense prevailed and we went home to sleep it off.

Newcastle Brown Ale is a strong brew and there were one or two other 'demob nights' where let's just say my memory is more than just a little hazy.

I still had a very sore head after the demob night out and the next day on leaving the barracks for the last time and going home in the train all on my own, I felt lonely and a bit sad. I thought a lot about my two years in the Forces and wondered what was ahead of me now.

It was a Thursday I was discharged and the next day I contacted British Rail whom I worked for before joining the Army.

I was interviewed and restarted my Railway career on Monday of the next week. The term 'sabbatical' was not in my vocabulary and anyway I needed money to live so I only had the weekend off before I started work again.

ON THE DUBLIN BOAT
1956

As a railway employee, at the age of seventeen, I took advantage of the free travel passes available to all railway workers. An employee, if I remember correctly, was entitled to one free pass per annum on most railway lines on the Continent including boat journeys across the English Channel to France and also the Burns and Laird boats from Glasgow to Belfast, Dublin and Derry.

In 1956, at the age of 17, I decided to use my free entitlement on a two-week holiday to Ireland. I had never been to Killarney and heard so much about it's beauty in song and legend. I thought I'd go there for myself and view its lakes and fells, as the popular song described. In fact, *'By Killarney's Lakes and Fells'* was the only song I ever heard my father sing even though, whilst he got the tune more or less ok, he just repeated the title over and over again.

This was a holiday I was taking completely on my own and no advance bookings of boarding houses or hotels were made prior to leaving. The itinerary was to sail from the Broomielaw in Glasgow to Dublin on the overnight Burns & Laird boat. Spend the weekend exploring Dublin and see all the sights of the Capital and then proceed by train to Killarney. Thereafter I would play it by ear but thought I would stop at one or two other places and then make for Bray just outside Dublin to spend the last week of the holiday. Bray was to Dublin, what Saltcoats was to Glasgow, a most popular seaside holiday resort. The only place I had ever been to in Ireland before then was Warrenpoint in County Down, on the Carlingford Lough. The stretch of water that separated the Republic of Ireland from the UK's Northern Ireland since the border was introduced in 1922. The Irish Free State consisted of 26 counties and the remaining six counties remained under British rule. Warrenpoint was the birthplace of my father, it is on the Northern side at the foot of the beautiful Mountains of Mourne and that is why we occasionally went to Warrenpoint.

The Burns and Laird Line boats from Glasgow, in addition to carrying passengers, also carried goods and cattle, so passengers booked to travel either 'First Class' or 'Steerage'. Thankfully our free passes warranted us entry to the First Class, which had lounges of sorts and of course a bar. I think there were a few cabins available but I just cannot remember whether I was allocated a cabin, but I do know I did not get a bed that night. Though I was only 17 years old and had not reached the legal age for consuming alcohol, there was a good going Irish sing-along taking place in the bar, so that's where I spent the night enjoying the company …and the Guinness.

After boarding the boat I naturally investigated everywhere I could on the vessel and that did not take too long. I went down to the lower deck to see what steerage passengers accommodation was like. As I said, these boats were used for carrying cattle and after each journey they would be hosed down to remove all the cow-shit. It did not however remove the smell, it was a horrible stench and I was so grateful that I did not have to spend the night in those quarters.

On my wandering around the boat I got into a conversation with an elegant, elderly gentleman with a beard. The decks were not very big so we met on two or three occasions on our walks and he was keen to know where I was going, where I worked, what my interests were. He was just a lovely, likeable old man and I enjoyed talking with him even though I felt so very inadequate speaking with, obviously, such a learned individual.

As the evening wore on the smell of the bar and sound of the singing gravitated me in the direction of the lounge and very soon I was part of the very friendly and gradually intoxicated company. There were many songs in which we all joined in but also a few solo performances. I even contributed one or two solos, *'Star of the County Down'* and *'Homes of Donegal'*, which was a new song at that time.

Included in the people at the tables around me, was an English sailor (not in uniform), a girl on her own, (I say a girl but at that time I was 17 and she was probably about 25 so to me she was not a girl, she was a woman). The others were mainly male and probably in the 50ish age group.

We had a thoroughly enjoyable evening and got to know each other fairly well. Eventually the bar closed and we all settled down to try and get some shuteye.

MAURICE WALSH - 'THE QUIET MAN'

I was up and about fairly early next morning and as we were sailing up the River Liffey to the docks I once again met the aforementioned elderly gentleman. He enquired of me where I was staying in Dublin and I told him that someone had given me the address of *The Sunshine Café* as a suitable B&B accommodation place. "My son will be meeting me at the docks in my car, so I will drop you off there as I know where it is".

Well I certainly didn't turn down that offer and when I saw the huge car I felt like a VIP being met at the boat. He tore a piece of paper, which he autographed and gave to me. It read;

"Yours Aye Maurice Walsh 19 V1 57".

He used the Roman numeral for June, which was fairly common with the older and more intellectual generation.

His autograph and photo can be seen in the photo section in the centre of the book.

At the time the name did not mean anything to me and he seems to have got the year wrong because it was 1956, I was not quite 18years old... or have I got the year wrong? Yeah it's probably me that has the date wrong.

When I returned home and told my brother John (who was the book-worm in the family) and showed him the autograph, he was beside himself with excitement. "That's Maurice Walsh", he said, "he wrote *'Key above the Door'* and *'The Quiet Man'* ... My God!"

I have often thought over the years that if I had told Mr. Walsh that I did not have a place to go to in Dublin and had to seek out a suitable accommodation, I feel that he would have offered me a room at his home, we got on so well together and he would have taken pity on me. I'll never know.

On researching this book, I googled *'Maurice Walsh'* and the photograph reproduced in this book is exactly how I picture him on the Glasgow to Dublin boat that day.

His book, *'The Quiet Man'*, was of course made into the classic film of the same name starring *John Wayne* and *Maureen O'Hara*, directed by *John Ford*, one of Hollywood's greatest directors in that era.

As promised, Mr. Walsh and his son conveyed me to the *Sunshine Café* and I spent two or three nights there, cannot remember exactly, but I do remember my 'bed and breakfast' accommodation, it was certainly memorable.

I shared a very large room up above the ground floor café, which had three double beds, yes three beds in the one room. There was no toilet or bathroom and showers in boarding houses were not heard of in Ireland at that time. What they provided were two basins with jugs of cold water on a dressing table for the purpose of washing and shaving (thankfully I didn't have a heavy growth and did not require to shave every day), we had the use of the toilet downstairs in the café and that was also where we got our breakfast... Not in the toilet of course.

The worst has still to come. I did not have the exclusive use of the double bed. I had to share this with another lodger, a total stranger. Now I wouldn't have complained if it had been a nice young colleen, but, no such luck, it was a middle aged man.

I introduced myself to the stranger... "Hello I'm Gerry". He responded... "Hi I'm Randy"

Well, that sure frightened me.

No, it's not true... I jest, but just the 'Randy' bit.

Probably the other double beds were similarly shared with strangers (and it was all males).

Now, in Ireland in the 1950s this was maybe considered quite normal in boarding houses. Unless you could afford to pay for a proper hotel then this was the norm, although I suppose you often would get the bed to yourself. However it was the summertime when I was there, so it was busy.

No toilet, no shower, no bath, no sink with running water, no privacy... NO WAY! I hear you all say.

Anyway, despite this, I thoroughly enjoyed my three nights in Dublin. The June weather was very nice and I spent a few pleasant sunshine hours in St. Stephen's Green.

I then got on the train for Killarney which was of course an old steam train, even more ancient than the ones I was working with at home.

On arrival in Killarney there was a man with a jaunting car who took me and my case to the Central Hotel in town. There were no taxis at the station but then it was nice to experience a jaunting car, a common mode of transport for short journeys around the town.

Well it only took me a day or so to take in the beautiful lakes and fells of Killarney but there was little else to interest a 17 year old, who was looking for dancing and lively entertainment, so a I got a train next day to the City of Cork.

KISSING THE BLARNEY STONE

I did get to a dance somewhere in the city as it was a Saturday night and would you believe the girl/woman who was in the drinking crowd in the bar on the boat coming over was also at the dance. We had a couple of dances but had she been about 7 or 8 years younger I may have had an extension to this story.

Next day was a Sunday and I went on a bus to visit the famed *Blarney Castle*. It wasn't over-commercialised at that time and there weren't any manicured gardens as there is today. Nor was there any charge to enter the castle and climb the many stairs up to the parapet where you could lie on your back and kiss *The Blarney Stone.*

There was a photographer there to take your photo kissing the stone and that was the only commercial aspect to the place. I ordered two photos, one taken on the ramparts, which I have, and one kissing the stone but one of my children must have snaffled that photo. I am waiting on the culprit owning up.

Because I left school half way through third year, my education was sadly neglected and in early adult life I really lacked confidence and felt inadequate when in the company of teachers, lawyers and such like due to my lack of eloquence and my inarticulacy.

Now, legend has it, that those who kiss the Blarney Stone are gifted with the power of eloquence. I'm not so sure the magic worked on me but when I consider the many occasions when I have been rabbiting on and been told to 'shut up', well maybe I did get a wee bit of the gift.

When I returned to Cork, after the Blarney visit, there was a massive religious procession through the city culminating in the Main Street. There, the Bishop celebrated Mass and Benediction, I think it was the Feast of Corpus Christi.

Everyone seemed to be in the procession, police, army, firemen, ambulance-men, scouts, nurses and lots of church sodalities and of course the general public. It seemed everyone in the city took part and it was not what I would ever expect to see in a catholic procession in Scotland, so it was quite amazing to me.

Next morning I took the train back up to Dublin with the intention of spending my second week in the seaside resort of Bray, at least I should get some dance halls and cinemas there.

I was walking from the railway station pacing the streets with my wee case in hand seeking out a bed and breakfast establishment. If it looked too posh I probably couldn't afford it and if it looked grubby I didn't want it. The money had to last me another week so I had to be very frugal. Frugal... that's all I ever was in my first 17 years.

Having met the girl from the boat when I was in Cork, now in Bray I bumped into another of the drinking party, none other than the English sailor. Such coincidences.

I explained that I was searching for accommodation and he gave me an address.

"I think they may be able to take you in", before parting he said, "by the way, some of that crowd from the boat are staying here and we are meeting tonight in Duffs pub".

He gave directions for the pub and said probably about 8 o'clock they'd all be there, so I said I would call in.

I went to the address he gave me and a very nice landlady opened the door and said she could take me for the week but would I mind sharing the bed with her son (who was 15 years old). The place looked very nice so I said Ok, deposited my case and had a wee cup of tea and a scone.

This place seems all right I thought… but still no bed to myself.

I duly turned up at Duff's pub and true enough there were a few men from the boat crowd and a wee sing-a-long was getting underway. Although I was not yet at the legal age for being served alcohol and I certainly didn't look older than my 17 years, no one seemed concerned.

Ten o'clock closing time came and went but we were all still there. The barman closed the door from the inside and continued to serve. Then he answered a knock on the door and two policemen joined the company and were soon imbibing with the rest of us, and joining in the songs.

It was probably approaching 11.15pm when the half inebriated party decided to disperse. The sailor said they, (he and two of the others), were going to a party at a house and invited me to accompany them. I was a bit apprehensive at the thought of gate crashing a party but he assured me that they would make me most welcome. The Guinness I had consumed influenced my decision to 'just go with it'.

To my great surprise, the house hosting the so called 'party' turned out to be the boarding house I had booked into. Well, the drinking and the singing continued for a few hours longer and in fact at 3am we were all sitting down at the table to enjoy a plate of fried eggs, chips and toast… Only in Ireland!

That was a great start to the week and I got on well with her son who had a job at the local fair ground for the holidays.

One of my most liked Irish singers and comedians at that time was a certain Joe Lynch. I owned his recording of *'Cottage by the Lee'*, a favourite Irish folk song of mine. A few years later, Joe appeared in a popular weekly sitcom on ITV Television, *'Never Mind the Quality, Feel the Width'*, which ran for about four years in the late 1960s. It was a comedy series about two tailors, one was a Jew, and Joe was the other; a the catholic Irishman. It was very funny and I imagine much of the content would today be considered 'Not PC'.

Joe was appearing at the local hall in Bray so I took the opportunity of enjoying his concert. I also had a few nights at the fair ground and the dance hall.

When I was saying goodbye to the lovely landlady after an enjoyable week in Bray, she confided in me that she had actually closed the spare room for redecoration… "Och, I just couldn't turn you away son". I was being pitied.

So ended my two week holiday of coincidences in Ireland… a holiday on my own… But was I on my own?

It's a true Irish saying *'A stranger is just a friend you've never met'.*

COURTING DAYS & MARRIAGE

In the 1950s, we didn't very often use the word 'courting'. More commonly, if you were dating or walking out together, the word used would be 'winching'. When boys were discussing girls they would want to know "Is she winching?"

As a teenager, one is in the pangs and torment of raging hormones, romantic feelings and sexual impulses and I was no different from the rest of the young lads. I certainly had my fair share of desires. From age 15 to 18, I was a booking clerk at Blairhill & Gartsherrie railway station in the steam train era. I knew every gorgeous looking girl who commuted to Glasgow and knew which train each of them came off.

I had to collect the tickets or check the weekly season tickets of all the passengers alighting from the train, so I always combed my hair, straightened my tie and put on a special smile, knowing which girl to expect.

Unfortunately, they would just rush right past me and not give me a second look... Damn it... Ach well, there was always another girl on the next train... or tomorrow night.

I did have a few dates with a couple of the girls at the station before I went into the Army for National Service.

My very first date, however, was with a girl I met at the Saturday night dancing at St Brides Hall in Motherwell.

Eating out at that time was a snack in the local café. This was before Reo Stakis came over from Cyprus, or was it Greece, and made it affordable for the man in the street to eat out at a proper restaurant.

His chain of restaurants hadn't reached Motherwell at that time, so after we left the cinema we went into the café in Merry Street and I ordered both of us a cup of tea and an 'exotic' plate of pie and beans with bread and butter. Wow! How romantic was that? A pie and beans was 9d after all.

Anyway, guess what happened then? I started to have a nosebleed. Oh Gawd, my first date and my nose starts to bleed. Jeezo! How embarrassing.

It did not seem, however, to worry the girl and we had a few more dates thereafter. There was a period of quite a few years when my nose would bleed at the most inconvenient of times. Usually at a works dance or other social functions. I think it was connected to some sort of nervousness on big occasions but I haven't had a nosebleed now for over 40 years, so I think it's safe to say that I have got over it. Is it hereditary? My son Gerard experienced the same for a time when he would have been about the same age as I was.

In a discussion with one of my grandsons, regarding entertainment in the 1950s, he just could not believe what a typical night out at the dancing or the cinema was like.

Every town had their regular weekly 'dancing at the palais' nights.

I often frequented Airdrie Town Hall and Coatbridge Town Hall where dances were held on Saturday nights. If I remember correctly, Mondays and Wednesdays were the other nights of the week that these dances were held.

The local palais was where one went to meet a partner. We would go with our pals hoping to impress and dance with a pretty girl and with a bit of luck she would fall for our patter and agree to be 'seen home', the common term for which was a 'lumber'.

Your friends and family would ask you, "Did you get a lumber last night?

This decision to ask to 'see her home' would be taken after due consideration of several factors which would have been established during conversations whilst dancing. Where does she live, can I get bus there and is there a bus back? Would this result in a long walk home? Would she reject my invitation? Is she pretty enough and worth any of these inconveniences?

Normally you would have had a few dances with her before you asked about a 'lumber' and near the end of the evening it would be the 'ladies choice' dance, affectionately referred to as 'the grab'. If she asked you up for that, then you knew you were in with a shout for a successful end to the evening.

What intrigued my grandson most was the format and practices at all the public dance halls.

The band would be on the stage at the top of the hall and the girls would congregate on one side and the men on the opposite side.

The bandleader would announce to "take your partners for the next quick step"

It was as though the girls were in a shop window display with the men walking up and down ogling from one to the other before deciding whom to approach 'requesting the pleasure of this dance'.

When I think back on it now it really must have been a bit degrading for the girls to be subjected to this 'inspection' before deciding whom to ask.

They could of course refuse the request but that was considered extremely impolite and frowned on. No matter how ugly he was, the girl would not embarrass him with a refusal.

If you were snubbed your mates would take pleasure in reminding you that you got the bum's rush.

Alcohol was not normally available at these dances and only soft drinks and crisps would be on sale during the short interval.

Dances usually finished by 10.30pm or 11pm at the latest but on holiday weekends there could be a late night dance starting at midnight and finishing about 3am. Invariably you would be walking home as there was no public transport at that hour and none of us had a car in the 1950s.

I remember one occasion when my friend Arthur and I went to a late dance in Coatbridge. We each seen a girl home (with a about a three mile walk to the outskirts of the town) and met again in the town centre. We then walked home to Calderbank, about another four miles, and it rained almost incessantly. Taxi?... that would never have been considered. We never had money for such luxuries.

Apart from the dance halls, the main entertainment alternative was the cinema.

A visit to the cinema in the 1940s and 50s usually involved standing in a queue on the pavement outside the theatre with a uniformed commissionaire controlling the queue.

Today you go to the cinema to see one film, but back then you were treated to the main feature film, another film (the 'B' movie), a selection of cartoons (Mickey Mouse, Popeye, etc.), trailers of forthcoming films and Pathe News. This was before we had TV at home so it was a source of seeing the news in live pictures from all over the world.

The interesting aspect of a night at the movies was that as it was so popular, queues could last for long periods. There was two 'houses' as each full performance was known, the first house and the second house.

As some people vacated the cinema the commissionaire would let others in but this meant that you were entering in the middle of a film. You then watched the remainder of the performance and eventually you got to see the first half of the movie on show when you entered the cinema.

"This is where we came in", we would say and therefore it was time to leave the cinema and let others enter.

It was crazy when you think about it, seeing the end of the film before the beginning, but what other option did we have.

I mentioned earlier that my closest pals from Calderbank were Arthur and Tom. Arthur was to be best man at his cousin Sadie's wedding who was marrying George, another of our friends from Calderbank. He was introduced to another Sadie, the bridesmaid, and a romance with Arthur and the bridesmaid soon began to blossom.

This was around Christmas 1959 and Arthur was taking Sadie to the Majestic Ballroom in Motherwell on Christmas night. He suggested that Tom and myself should meet Sadie and accompany him to the Majestic.

"Two of Sadie's sisters will be with her" he said, "Susan and Rena, I think you two should meet them". He was just trying to play 'matchmaker', I thought.

I was home on Christmas leave from the Army and was due to be de-mobbed about five weeks later in February.

We went along with his suggestion but before going in to the Majestic, we had a few pints in 'The Hairy Man's Pub', just across the street from the ballroom.

After the dance we all took the bus to 'see the girls home' to their house in Newarthill. Well that really was the start of relationships that were destined to last for the remainder of all our lives. Tom matched up with Susan and I was, undoubtedly, the most fortunate to become romantically involved with Rena.

Within about three years, we three pals from Calderbank, married three (of six) sisters from Newarthill and these three couples and all their children have had a very close relationship throughout their lives.

I have made many good decisions in my life but easily the greatest of all was to ask Rena to marry me. Apart from giving birth to our four outstanding, talented, responsible children who have all turned out to be exemplary adults way beyond our expectations, no one could wish for a partner with all the qualities and attributes which Rena has.

In addition to that, she was, and still is, incredibly beautiful. What did I do to deserve Rena, I often ask myself.

She told me that it was her intention to become a nun before she met me... she wanted to be married to God. Well, I told her she got the next best thing.

At this point I will say that Rena is, deep down, a very shy and also a very private person. She never seeks the limelight and I know that, in this book, she would be embarrassed and unhappy if I say too much about things she would consider private and personal. So in deference to her wishes, I will be very careful here and just relate a select few of my memories where Rena is concerned.

Arthur Tom and I, all had about three courting years before marriage and so we were constantly in each other's company.

It was about a four or five mile walk from Calderbank to Newarthill and several nights a week, one, two or all three of us would be trudging the return road, unless we caught the last bus on that route at 10.20pm.

Very often, due to inclement weather, especially snow, we would just stay overnight instead of walking home, so the three boys in a bed or on the bed-settee, was a common occurrence.

The house in Newarthill was one of Weir's steel houses. These homes were of steel construction and steel clad and subject to much condensation. I don't know what kind of insulation there was, if any, but they were extremely cold in the winter.

There wasn't any central heating but there was a fireplace in the sitting room and the main bedroom. The other rooms had no heating at all.

The winter of 1962 was one of the coldest on record and the room on the gable end was the coldest. By morning the ice on the inside of the window could sometimes be over one inch thick…ON THE INSIDE.

I remember one night that winter, Arthur, Tom and I shared a bed in that room. The girls laid claim to every available hot water bottle, so we filled some Iron Brew bottles with boiled water as substitutes and they were greatly appreciated.

You will realise just how cold it was in that room when I tell you that in the morning, even though the bottles were under the blankets all night, the water inside the bottles had turned into ice. That is a true fact.

It was the equivalent of sleeping in a freezer. There was steam when you exhaled your breath, which of course was condensation. I had to sleep with my head under the blankets even though I felt smothered, at least my nose and eyes didn't freeze over.

I recall one incident on a dark Saturday night, well about 1am it was, Arthur and I were about a mile and a half out of Newarthill on the way home when I thought I saw something strange lying on the grass verge at the side of the road.

I glanced again and the hair on the back of my neck stood up.

"Arthur, look"...

It was the body of a man, motionless.

"Jesus, is he dead?"

We crept close to him, suspecting that he was perhaps just drunk.

"He's not breathing Arthur, there's not a sound".

"Oh God, if he's dead we better not touch him".

We took a few paces onwards and stopped again, went back and got a bit closer to him... still no sound of breathing.

"We better phone the police".

Now, this was about 30 years before mobile phones came on the scene but we knew we would be passing a phone box about a mile or so further on at Newhouse Industrial Estate, just beside the cottage at Legbrannock where James Kier Hardie, founder of the Labour Party, was born. So we could phone the police from there.

We duly phoned 999 and the police arranged to pick us up at the phone box to take them to the body. It seemed to be taking ages for them to arrive, at least half an hour had elapsed since we discovered the body.

"You know, maybe that bugger is just drunk and sleeping it off".

"Maybe he's woken up by this time and went on his way".

We were getting worried by this time.

"Aye, we're gonnae look like right eejits, we don't even know exactly where he was".

These thoughts were going through our minds when the police car arrived and we got in, emphasising to them that he may have disappeared by now, and we drove off.

Ah relief, the cars lights beamed onto the body, he's still there at least, dead or alive.

The two cops went over to the man, at first they also thought he was dead.

After a few moments they decided to shake him, a couple of rough shakes and the body wakened from its comatose state and uttered...

"Haw, whit is it, hey, ye gave me a fright there".

"Not as big a fright as you gave us", said the cop, "Get up and get on your way"

146

How drunk he was, if at all, we don't know, but we were just glad he was still alive.

The police were kind enough to give us a lift as far as the A8 at the other side of Newhouse but any further was beyond their territory, so we had to walk the last mile or so.

Post war housing was still a big problem so when we got married we moved in to a bedroom in my mother's house.

About nine months and two weeks after the wedding, our first-born child, Gerard, arrived. We didn't waste too much time in the Grant family to contribute to the human race. I was at the birth of all four of our children and in 1964 fathers were not really encouraged to be at the birth.

Another incident I remember, Rena and I were just married and living in a room in my Mother's house and my father's small room was opposite our room.

My father always had a glass of whisky on the table next to his bed, beside an ashtray.

He smoked in bed too, mixing drink and smoking in bed is not a good idea. One night, about two o'clock in the morning, he came into our room and shook me.

"Gerard, I've set the bed on fire, don't waken the others".

That's a nice greeting when someone wakens you in the middle of the night. I went into his room, the bed was not 'on fire' as such, but the hair mattress was smouldering and emitting smoke though not really as much as I thought it should have when I saw the size of the area affected. It was about 15 inches in diameter. I just got a kettle of water and ensured that the smouldering was extinguished and safe. He must have been wakened either by the heat or the smoke but that could have been a disastrous night. It's frightening to think of it even now.

We stayed at my mother's house for about a year but with a baby, Rena, naturally, preferred to be with her own mother. There was now a spare room there since Sadie and Susan were married and left the house, so we moved to Newarthill.

A couple of incidents while living in Newarthill are worthy of mention. One Saturday night with snow and sleet falling, there was a loud knock on the door. It was just after midnight, Rena and I had been in bed for no more than a couple of hours, she was a nurse and was due on early shift the next morning.

Her mother was the only one still up, the living room light was on and that's why there was a knock on the door.

She answered it to find a young fellow of about 17 or 18 with blood on his head and face, he pleaded with her to take him in to avoid a gang who were chasing him. He was from the Bellshill area and had been at a dance locally but got picked on by some young thugs.

Rena's mother was a compassionate person and of course took the lad in and closed the door.

She sat the lad in a chair, "You sit there son, that cut will need attended to".

She then called on Rena to get up and treat the patient. I too was on the floor in my pyjamas, thinking, what the hell's going on here.

The boy was cleaned and a plaster put on the head wound and given a cup of tea. After a wee while we decided it would be safer if he got a taxi to get home rather than walk to Bellshill. There was no phone in the house, so I had to put on some clothes over my pyjamas and a coat and hat then take the lad down to the nearest phone box, about 100 yards past Newarthill Cross.

I thought to myself while walking with him, 'maybe this gang are still waiting on him reappearing'. I was extremely apprehensive but thankfully there was no sign of anyone at that time on a cold damp and snowy night.

We heard the sound of breaking glass before we reached the Main Street and when we turned the corner and passed one of the shops, a drapers, I noticed that their shop window was smashed in and glass spread on the pavement.

That must have been the smash noise we heard a few moments earlier, so after I phoned for the taxi I phoned the police to report the broken window.

148

That Monday night, when I got the Evening Times at Glasgow Central station on my way home, I read that a man had appeared in court that day regarding a break-in at the shop in Newarthill on Saturday night. I cannot remember what sentence or fine he got but shortly after that I received a letter of commendation from the Chief Constable of Lanarkshire County Constabulary, praising me for reporting the incident.

They caught the culprit red handed. He had just left the shop, carrying the swag, when the police arrived.

In my research for this book, up in the loft, I came across the letter from the Chief Constable, which reads:

Dear Sir,

It has been reported to me that about 2.30am on Saturday 20th March 1965, you observed that the display window of the shop at 150 High Street, Newarthill, had been smashed. You immediately initiated a '999' call and as a result the police were quickly on the scene. They apprehended a man a short distance from the shop in possession of drapery goods.

On Monday 22nd March 1965, the man appeared at the Sherriff Court Hamilton, charged with theft by housebreaking and was sentenced to six months imprisonment.

I wish to place on record my appreciation of your public spirited action and co-operation with the police on this occasion.

Yours faithfully,

John Wilson
Chief Constable

Rena's mother had great devotion to the Virgin Mary and she had a large statue of Our Lady of Lourdes contained in a large glass globe. This sat on top of the radiogram in the sitting room. Her mother would kneel in front of this statue to say her morning prayers and if the radiogram was playing she would of course switch it off.

One of the presents I got from my railway colleagues when we got married was a small transistor radio, a recent invention at the time. It worked by batteries and measured only about 3inches by 5 inches and about 1inch thick.

Rena and I and our son Gerard, were living in a room at her mothers house and I used to switch the transistor on in the morning getting ready to leave for work and sit it on top of the radiogram.

On this particular morning Rena had come home from night shift at the hospital and soon went to bed. It appears that I forgot to switch off the transistor radio.

When her mother got up to start her housework she switched off the radiogram so that she could say her prayers.

She did not realize that the sound was coming from the transistor, therefore, although she turned the switch on and off, again and again, the radio was still playing music.

She was dumbfounded as to why it didn't go off.

She then moved the radiogram away from the wall to remove the plug from the socket. That will surely switch it off, depriving it of power. No, it didn't of course, because it was the transistor that was playing.

'Mother of God, what are you doing to me' she thought, 'is this some sort of miracle'.

In desperation, despite Rena being asleep after a night shift, she wakened her and related the mystery of the miraculous radiogram.

Rena of course saw the transistor and realised why her mother was in such a state and showed her the offending transistor radio.

"That wee bugger has done that to me", she said, blaming me for her terrible upset.

'That wee bugger', was her term of affection for her favourite son-in-law and always called me that when I played any prank on her... and I did play a few.

MY GOLF HANDICAP... ME

As a young person I never thought I would ever be on a golf course. Golf was the sport for the rich, not the working class, but when we moved down to Irvine I found that things were a bit different down there. In fact, on the Ayrshire coast from Irvine down to Ayr there are more golf courses in an area that size than anywhere else in the world and the working classes also participated in the sport.

Beside Irvine Golf Course there was a little mining village of just a few houses called Bartonholm.

It doesn't exist anymore but from that village there were three golfers who became Scottish Amateur Champions, Hammy McInally, Jack Carson and Jimmy Walker. Hammy actually won the Scottish Amateur title three times.

They all became members of the Irvine Golf Club, which is very proud of those three Bartonholm golfers.

I first played a round of golf on the Irvine Ravenspark Municipal Golf Course.

When I say played, that's a bit of an exaggeration, even with the encouragement and tuition of 'good golfer' friends plus perseverance and practice, I never achieved any level of proficiency.

I did enjoy the fresh air, and walking, of course, is a great exercise.

If, on a normal 18 hole golf course the average player will walk about five miles, I reckon my average is nearer nine miles when you take into consideration the slice shots, the hook shots, the out of bounds on the adjacent fairways and the yardage covered in searching for lost balls.

I did become a member at Ardeer Golf Club in Stevenston.

Most club members would participate in the monthly medal and strive to reduce their handicap. Not once, in the few years of membership at the club, did I take part in the 'medal'. It would have been far too embarrassing for me and even more frustrating for my golf partners.

I mostly played, therefore, either by myself or with one or two of my brother-in-laws. I hastily add that they were even worse golfers than me.

We started playing in the early 1970s and at that time the Concorde supersonic jet aircraft training flights were being performed at Prestwick Airport. I recall a number of occasions when on the golf course we would stop and stare up to the sky in admiration and awe at the sight of the Concorde in flight. It was worth going on to the golf course just for the uninterrupted view of this aviation icon.

There were two incidents on the golf course at Ardeer that stand out in my memory.

The first one was on a very cold and windy November day.

There was or had been a covering of frost, so why we ventured out to endure these conditions I just cannot explain. Lets just say it was a Saturday afternoon and that was the only day of the week we were not working, so 'we were going to enjoy our day on the course, come hell or high water'.

It was my brother-in-law Tom who accompanied me that day. We were preparing to tee off at the 8th and directly in front of this tee was a fast flowing burn (due to heavy rain that week).

That burn, in itself, was a psychological hazard to both of us as, invariably, our first shot would land in the burn but that didn't bother us that day.

On the other side of the burn, there was a path which led to a wooden sleeper bridge over the burn and there was a golfer, pulling his trolley behind him, passing in front of our tee.

We courteously paused to let him pass and watched him attempt to cross on the sleeper bridge.

With the frost, one has to be careful when stepping on the wooden sleepers, as it is so easy to slip on that surface. He kind of cut the corner going on to the bridge and his golf trolley wheel didn't quite make it and began to slide down the banking. He swung round and tried to save his trolley from entering the burn, in vain.

He wouldn't let go of the handle and gravity pulled the trolley into the burn. We could not believe our eyes. He didn't have the sense to release his grip on the trolley and so he followed it in.

He was almost up to his knees in water when he managed to get to his feet again.

Now, I know it is most unkind to laugh at other people's misfortune, very unkind.

However, we could not contain ourselves. We sort of turned away from his direction hoping he would not hear our laughter and sniggering. It was actually painful attempting to suppress our hilarity.

We could not believe his stupidity and yet we truly felt extremely sorry for him. The water must have been ice cold and his clothes soaked through.

He just lifted his trolley on to the bridge, climbed out and went on his merry, well not so merry, way.

He must have been physically shivering by the time he got to the clubhouse. Surely he didn't continue to play. We didn't stare after him to avoid his embarrassment.

A CHANCE IN A MILLION!

The second incident only involved myself.

There was a series on TV called 'A Chane in A Million', or a title similar to that, which portrayed the most unlikely of coincidences. The following incident would I'm sure have qualified to be featured on that show.

I did not use a golf trolley as I was always fit enough to carry my bag in those days and I had the habit of clipping my car keys onto the top of the bag somewhere.

I played the 18 holes on my own but when I got to the 4th tee I sliced my shot, really wild.

To the right of this fairway was the green of the 8th hole and there were 3 or 4 golfers on that green. Now to be honest, I had hit a good strong shot and if it had went in the right direction I would have been truly proud of my drive but it was a slice and it landed on the 8th green.

It bounced once and then struck one of the golfers. My shout of "Fore" was either not heard or he did not see the offending ball approach. I'm happy to say that the bounce had taken a lot of the sting out of the shot and he did not sustain any injury. I profusely apologised to the man, apart also from being so embarrassed at my atrocious golfing ability.

I continued to play the remainder of the holes and eventually got back to the car to go home.

I went for my keys, which I had clipped on the top of the bag, but to my dismay they were not there. Shit!!

They must have fallen off at some point perhaps when I dropped the bag to take a shot... But where? There's about 5 miles of distance to cover that course but the slicing etc. added another couple of miles to my journey. Hell!

There's nothing else for it but to retrace my every shot at every hole. Now you may think, if you don't play golf, 'how would you remember all your strokes?'. Incredibly, I think most golfers easily remember, especially when it is immediately following the round.

So I started to cover the 18 holes again, searching carefully around everywhere that I paused and dropped my bag. I may add at this point, I found a ball, which I had lost at the 3rd tee, one of a few I lost that day, which is par for the course for me.

When I got to the 4th tee I glanced to the right and thought this is where I attacked that other unfortunate golfer with my stray ball, so I made my way to the 8th green where the offence took place.

When I got there I stood at the edge of the green and waited until two players tee'd off on the 4th tee.

Then the incredible 'chance in a million' incident took place! The second player to tee off shouted "Fore", I did not see the ball at all but believe me I felt it!

It hit me on the wrist and also hit the winder on my favourite Tissot watch.

A huge lump quickly appeared on my wrist and later turned black and blue. This ball did not bounce first so I got the full force of the projectile.

The winder on my watch had to be replaced and though I love that watch it has never worked properly since. To be honest that fact hurt me more than the damage to my wrist.

So there you have it, I tee off on the 4th and hit someone on the 8th green. That in itself is really not such a common occurrence, but for someone else to tee off on the 4th and hit me on the 8th green on the very same day? I ask you, what are the odds?

Now, perhaps you have forgotten by this time but the purpose of re-tracing my moves was to search for my missing car keys. I completed all 18 holes but sadly could not find them.

I was back at the car by then and thought I'll have to phone home and ask Rena to come and rescue me. There were no mobile phones in those days and I was just about to enter the clubhouse and use the public phone when I thought 'I'll check the golf bag one more time'. Just to be absolutely sure, I actually removed all the golf clubs and then turned the bag upside down.

A few spare balls and tees and pencils fell out and then… Yeah, you've guessed it the keys were inside the bag all this time. Why the hell did I not think of doing that in the first place?

I have already emphasised that I am not good at golf. If I do manage to get the odd par 3 or par 4 I am truly elated. If I get two or even three holes in par, I consider that is indeed a good golf day.

The sport for me was an opportunity for exercise and also as a social occasion with a few of my friends.

Arthur, is one of my brother-in-laws and he and I throughout our life, even from childhood, have been very competitive with one another.

Whether it be playing headers, snooker, cards or whatever, we each earnestly want to be the winner.

I know this will annoy him for me to say this, but I was better than he at absolutely everything we played, he may disagree of course.

In the sport of golf, we were both hopeless.

One of Arthur's regular waterholes in Kilwinning was The Lemon Tree and each year they had a golf outing, usually to Girvan. Although their annual outing went under the pseudonym of a golf outing, an all day long piss up was a much truer description.

It started off with bacon rolls and pints (pints plural) in the pub then the bus to Girvan and naturally you needed a few drams of whisky to combat the boredom of the journey.

On arrival at the Girvan Golf club one had of course to sample the local beer, with a sausage roll or pie or maybe another bacon roll. (Gawd, this is sure putting me in the mood, I can smell the bacon)

Then we were all given our scorecards with your handicap indicated thereon.

Arthur and I, as you would expect, got the maximum handicap permitted. I think it was 18, or maybe 21.

Now normally, even if I had double that handicap, I would not have been in contention to finish in the first three or ten.

However, there was some sort of sporting miracle that day and I played the best day of golf I ever did in my life. As I said it was a miracle.

Maybe it was the Girvan beer or something in the bacon rolls but I surpassed myself on that course. I don't remember what the final tally of strokes was but I actually won the cup that day and I think it was by 2 or 3 strokes.

It did not please some of the 'real' golfers on the outing. I actually was a bit embarrassed in being presented with the cup, which I understand was the last occasion that this cup was competed for... were they so dismayed?

My delight on the outcome was matched only by the envy and disappointment of Arthur.

He was never allowed to forget that day and his accusations that I somehow falsified the scorecard were vehemently denied.

PET HATES OF A GRUMPY OLD MAN

My favourite drinking mug at present is one that has the message printed on it 'Grumpy Old Man', a gift on some Fathers Day from one of my daughters.

Well, maybe I am at times a wee bit grumpy, but it is not without cause and my response to those accusing me of grumpiness is that, at my age and experience, I have earned the right to be grumpy and, I suppose, it is maybe true to say that I don't suffer fools gladly.

I look around and observe so many things going on which irritate and annoy me and I cannot help commenting on and complaining about them.

Some of these things are very trivial and I shouldn't really get myself worked up about them so let's just call them a few of my 'pet hates':

1. Long Laces

I'll start with laces. Laces that are almost twice the length they need be, especially with trainers, which incidentally I find very comfortable.

When they are fully laced up I find that I still have enormous lengths remaining and so I have to tie them in bows. Bows plural, because one bow still has them trailing on the ground and is a safety hazard, which could result in nasty trip.

Has anyone worked out how much the NHS would save if they didn't have to treat accidents caused by tripping on laces that are too long?

A minimum of two bows are necessary and two bows looks so stupid, but more importantly, unnecessary.

Countless millions of laces are manufactured every year and most are about 30% longer than required. Surely some bean counter can advise the manufacturers of the savings their companies could make with this simple change.

When I get a new pair of trainers I often remove the laces and cut the superfluous length off... then I have one end with an aglet and the other end that ravels; another source of annoyance!

2. Buttons on Your Flies

As a boy and a teenager my trouser fly was generally fastened with buttons. Then the great invention of a zipper was introduced and it was so much easier and convenient.

Button-fly trousers more or less disappeared. That was until some 'fashion minded' designer decided that we should all step back in time and reintroduce the button-fly. "You have to be in the fashion", they said. Well I say, "stuff your fashion!". So many times I have eventually found the jeans or trousers that seem perfect on me and then I discover the dreaded buttons... shit!

Do I walk away or do I take them and ensure many instances of frustration

I have a really nice pair of jeans, perfect in every way... except the button-fly! After much deliberation I relented and took them. Whilst I do like them, what should normally be the simple operation of a quick nip into the toilet to relieve myself after one or two glasses of refreshment, it is somewhat embarrassing to do a partial striptease act just for a wee pee.

To add to the annoyance, I often have difficulty inserting the buttons. Gawd, whit eejit thought these were a good idea?

3. Salt Shakers

Salt shakers and pepper shakers, in the first 50 years of my life, were simple and straightforward.

You lifted the shaker and you shook it over the meal. Nothing could be easier. But then this 'fashion thingy' reared its ugly head again.

The manufacturers came out with... 'Impress your dinner guests with the fashionable and attractive salt and pepper grinders. Easy to grip and featuring an adjustable grinder to meet your preferences'... Jeez O!

Some now are about 12 inches high, we even have a set at home with lights on them, if you can work out how to operate them. Needless to say I didn't buy them.

It really irritates me when I'm invited for dinner and I'm faced with a set that I know I'm going to have trouble with.

I lift it up and try shaking it over the dish... NAW! I try the other end... NAW! I try twisting one end... still NAW!

"You need to take the lid off" ... "Oh, I see"... Right, that's fine, now do I shake or twist?...What end dispenses the salt, or is this the pepper?... It's the salt I want... For God's sake, my dinner is getting cold.

4. The 'Designer' Label

If the manufacturers put the word 'designer' on their product they think they are guaranteed to increase sales at extortionate prices.

Why does Joe Public fall for all these advertising gimmicks? You're not in the 'in crowd' if you don't have this latest whatever.

They even have designer bottled water. Water is colourless, odourless and tasteless, so who can tell the difference. So many times I have seen on TV that in all the tests that have been carried out, ordinary tap water in Scotland comes out tops and is safer.

OK, when you go to Spain and other places it is more pleasant to drink the bottled water and you feel safer so doing, but I'm sure their tap water is also safe enough.

To get back to designer wear, clothing, handbags, watches etc. The fake designer industry is really big business and whilst at first glance or even close inspection most people find it difficult to differentiate the fake from the genuine article, probably the quality will tell in wear through time. But is it worth so much more?

The so-called designer jeans truly amazes me and some people are prepared to pay several hundred ££s for an item made with common denim. There seems to be no limit to what some customers will pay for the latest label or style.

So that is another of my pet hates … the word, 'Designer'.

For everyday use, I wear a cheap watch I got on sale on the cruise ships for about $10 to $20, and it keeps perfect time. Rena and I each have a Tudor Oyster watch, made by Rolex, but less expensive. Our children gave Rena and I these watches as a silver wedding gift in 1988 and even then, they cost our children over £1000 each. A few years ago it cost over £300 just to have mine serviced and cleaned… and it still doesn't operate properly.

On the subject of jewellery, the man in the street cannot tell the difference between genuine diamonds and cubic zirconia so I would go for Cubic zirconia… well, I am a self-confessed cheapskate, a product of the austere 1940s.

"No one can tell the difference", I say to Rena in the hope that the cheaper sparkling version will suffice.

"Yes, but I will know, and that's what matters" she says… so I never win.

5. Blister Packs

Medicine pills come in blister packs and I have no dispute with them. They are quite easy and safe to open.

The kind of blister packs I have a quibble with are those small items, very often light bulbs, that are encased in a hard clear plastic bubble type pack.

I have cut myself several times over the years in attempting to get to the contents. These packs are definitely dangerous and there is never any hazard notice or printed instructions on how to open them.

I have learned from experience now, to not even attempt to open by hand, or teeth, and just reach for the scissors and hope I don't destroy the contents.

6. Foreign Call Centres

I think I am in the majority here when I complain about 'Customer Care Centres' based in the India.

Now, I am very fond of our Asian friends and simply adore a nice strong curry but on the telephone I often cannot understand clearly what they are saying.

It is partly my fault in that I don't have perfect hearing, in fact I sometimes wear hearing aids.

I maintain that it is not that I cannot hear the sounds, it's just that I cannot decipher the words. Therefore, I blame the speaker, who may benefit from elocution lessons.

Better still the customer care call centres should provide these jobs at home and not overseas.

7. Meals on a Flight

Crammed into an economy seat on an aircraft is, in itself, quite hellish. Trying to eat a three-course meal in these conditions is just impossible. I no longer even attempt it.

I try to take on board a roll with bacon or salmon and a carton of milk. I can handle that, and so avoid spilling much of my dinner and tea over myself, or a neighbouring passenger.

Who needs to eat anyway on a 2 or 3 hour flight? It's not worth the inconvenience. Now, if they would only give me a free upgrade to First Class...

8. Running out of Toilet Roll

Now this is something that NEVER EVER happens in our home. Rena ensures that there is a supply in each toilet cupboard to last a minimum of 6 months. It is embarrassing to be faced with this problem in someone else's home or in a public toilet. 'Now, why didn't I check first?'

9. Miscellaneous Pet Hates

Without going into any detail, these are a number of other things that bring out the grumpiness in me and I'm sure many of you, my dear readers:

Slow internet connections,

Cold telephone callers,
Security checks at airports (I know, it really is essential, but a bloody
nuisance),
People smoking in my company,
Expensive car parking charges,
Car parking places, which are suitable only for 'Smart' Cars,
Stepping on chewing gum or dog poo on public paths or pavements.
Oh, I forgot, I hate tripe and hate kidneys.

A CAREER IN THE MEDIA

I am not going to bore readers with a comprehensive chronological record of employment but suffice to say that I have had a varied career and a very enjoyable working life. I more or less drifted into jobs and then progressed in various fields rather than any kind of planned career.

From a railway booking clerk I got a promotion to selling advertising space on railway property and on buses.

British Transport Advertising came under the jurisdiction of British Railways and that was my introduction into the advertising sales profession, which really governed my working life thereafter.

From there, I moved into press advertising sales with the Glasgow Herald, a subsidiary of George Outram & Co. who, at that time, were buying up titles of local press in Scotland.

They had just purchased The Kilmarnock Standard and although I was only a short time with the Herald, the bosses were very satisfied with my success and asked me to move to the Standard in Kilmarnock, to improve the advertising in that title.

I was living in Irvine then, so it was much closer to home and presented a challenging opportunity.

Soon afterwards, I was asked to include *The Ayrshire Post* in my responsibilities, then the group purchased the Irvine Herald and that also came under my management.

In addition to being responsible for the advertising sales, circulation and promotions, office management tasks were added to my remit. When I started in newspapers in Ayrshire they were produced by hot metal typesetting, producing lines of type moulded in lead, but modernisation introduced web-offset printing. Oh, what a difference that was. I have many great memories of my time in Newspapers but it would be of little interest to most people, so I will only highlight some incidents.

The 1980s was the time that 'free-sheet' newspapers were coming on the scene. I had often seriously thought that I would have been successful in such a venture but was reluctant to gamble my livelihood and that of my wife and four children, so I dismissed the thought.

There did, however, come the opportunity when the newspaper group I worked with engaged in mass reorganisation and offered redundancy packages to all employees.

I talked things over with all the family and decided to take the gamble of becoming self-employed.

It turned out to be a great career move. I started my own free newspaper covering Ardrossan, Saltcoats and Stevenston, with a 15,000 distribution.

I gave the publication the title of *'The Three Towns Trader'*.

I say newspaper, but of course it did not carry news as such. It was, basically, an advertising publication and any free space was filled with competitions, quizzes, photographs and of course advertising features on businesses, shops and events.

It was only published every four weeks and from its first issue it was very successful, much to the dislike of the local press. It was a 'one man show', with a little help from members of the family.

I arranged the distribution to all the houses in the Three Towns and to organise that project I required a local street map. There was not an up to date street plan for the area available at that time, so using my entrepreneurial skills I produced and published a street plan of the three towns.

Photos of the front cover can be seen in the centre section of this book. When the artwork was completed, I took it to the local Council to request if it could be published, with the approval of 'Cunninghame District Council', with that imprint on the front cover. They agreed.

Not missing a chance to make an extra buck or two, I sold advertising spaces surrounding the map. I cannot remember the number of copies I had printed, possibly about 500, but they sold out very quickly and I ordered a reprint.

It was quite gratifying for me to see just how many of the commercial businesses in the area had this street plan pinned on their office walls. As I had teams of mainly school kids doing the distribution of the Three Towns Trader, I offered a leaflet distribution service alongside the free paper and it gave the kids an opportunity to earn a bit extra. That aspect of the business was quite successful too.

My 'free sheet' publication was printed in Carlisle as at that time the print trade unions in Scotland 'blacked' free sheets not connected with paid-for titles.

I would have been much happier and have had less travelling if I could have had it printed locally but the strong unions prevented that. In the second year of publication I added the village of West Kilbride to my distribution.

THE LARGS CHRISTMAS SHOPPER

To test the market in Largs, I produced two, 4-page, pre Christmas, advertising publications under the title 'Largs Christmas Shopper', for distribution in the town.

This did not go down well with the local paper, the Largs & Millport Weekly News, whose parent company was the Ardrossan & Saltcoats Herald.

They published a front-page story insinuating that I was some kind of fly-by-night businessman coming up from England to fleece local traders and run back down south.

I was well known in newspapers in Ayrshire and I'm sure they were well aware of who this 'businessman' was. They just did not like the competition.

To be fair, I was taking advantage of an inexpensive way of providing an advertising medium to the local traders without giving anything back to the community. I admit that, but we live in a capitalist world and the traders got good value for money by advertising in my free sheet.

One of my major advertisers in the Three Towns Trader was also a major customer of the Ardrossan & Saltcoats Herald.

He was very angry at the 'story' on the front page of their Largs newspaper and as he was advertising in both of my publications, he felt that any bad publicity could have an adverse affect on his business if he was associating with this dodgy 'fly-by-night entrepreneur from England'.

He contacted the Herald and demanded that they print a retraction of the story about me, and my Christmas issues in Largs, he also suggested that I write to the editor pointing out all the inaccuracies in their article.

I followed his advice and sent a letter to the editor, explaining the true facts, which they published two weeks later. However, alongside my letter the editor published his note, still griping and repeating inaccuracies. I'm sure their readers would consider it to be just 'sour grapes'.

My Three Towns Trader publication was published only every four weeks so this gave me time to introduce other ventures, one of which was vinyl lettering signs for shop windows, vans, notice boards etc. I also did the annual championship boards at Irvine Bogside Golf Club and some bowling clubs.

I asked a friend of mine who was the accountant in the newspaper group we both previously worked with, to be my accountant and do my tax returns.

The first year's tax return showed a reasonable profit and he remarked to me, "Any new business start-up is not expected to make a profit

until about the third year. I've included every kind of cost I can think
of and you have still made a big profit in your first year".
I continued with the free newspaper for about four years until just
after I became a Sub Postmaster.

SUB-POSTMASTER VENTURES

In my capacity as Advertisement Manager with the newspaper group
which included The Ayrshire Post, Kilmarnock Standard and Irvine
Herald, I made many contacts and one was a Cumnock man who had
a variety of business ventures including newsagents, sub post offices
and a cash and carry warehouse.
I always had a wee notion to run a sub post office and he gave me an
insight into the ramifications involved. In due course, I purchased a
sub office in Main Street in Ayr, which was one of the busiest in the
County.
Being appointed as a sub postmaster was a bit complicated and took a
fair length of time and while I was waiting to hear if I was successful
in my application another sub office in Ayr was advertised, I applied
for that too, in case I did not get the Main Street one.
The head postmaster in Ayr told me, when he was welcoming me to
my position of sub postmaster, that if I hadn't got the Main Street office I would definitely have got the other one, in Whittlets, Ayr.
In those days, the sub offices handled a great deal of cash, paying out
family allowances and retirement pensions, so post office burglaries
were commonplace throughout the nation.
After about a year or so in the position, there was a break-in overnight
at the Whittlets Post Office, the one I would have got had I been un-
successful with the Main Street office.
The assailants forced entry through the night and when the postmaster
opened up the door in the morning he was very brutally attacked with
a hammer or some such implement.
He received serious injuries and was in hospital for a lengthy period.

I thought, 'Oh God, that could have been me'. My guardian angel must have been looking after me again.

I got to thinking however, if a robbery attempt similar to the Whittlets office were to be made at my Sub Post Office, I should start to take some precautions and devise a warning system.

The rear of the office was a low roof, lean-to small room and any burglars would find this the easiest method of entry. A sliding door gave access from this small room to the main part of the office and so that door would require to be opened by any potential thieves.

It was stipulated that we had to leave the room light on 24 hours, which meant that there was a clear view from the street windows of the entire office, except the small room.

I devised a system that if the door was slid open, even just a couple of inches, it would move an item that would not return to its position and thereby I would know that an illegal entry had been effected.

Each morning when my daughter Maureen and I arrived, I did not unlock the main door until I checked that the sliding door had not been disturbed. If it had been, I would have contacted the police immediately and let them be the first to go into the shop. Thankfully my security system was not put to the test.

When I bought the Ayr Main Street Sub Post Office there was no other business operating from the premises but I soon introduced greetings cards, stationery, confectionery and later a trophy and engraving business. In the photo section of the book there is a photograph of the shop-front. All the sign work was procured and affixed by myself, an example of my 'signs' business.

I then bought another Sub Post Office in Kilmarnock. This one also had a newsagent and licensed grocer business attached, my son Gerard and an assistant was employed to manage that one.

I soon realised however that this was a wrong move.

The post office was in a deprived area of the town and there were a number of undesirables who frequented the shop.

In 2011, BBC Scotland screened a BAFTA Award-winning documentary entitled 'The Scheme', comprising a series of six episodes, following the lives of some families in the Onthank and Knockinlaw housing scheme in Kilmarnock.

This was the area I had the Post Office. It was in fact called 'Knockinlaw Post Office' and was featured in the TV series.

Whilst there were very many good kind people using the shop there was a constant worry of the undesirable element in the community. Break-ins in the area and violence was not uncommon, so after only a few months I put the business up for sale.

Within nine months of purchase I had sold the business. Nevertheless, I did make a wee profit in the buying and selling transactions.

I was still doing my free newspaper and leaflet distribution service and my signs for shops and vans.

I owned two sub post offices and related businesses and my trophy and engraving business was really taking off.

It was all getting a wee bit stressful, especially with the amount of cash that was being handled and I think a combination of all these things was, perhaps, the main cause of the heart attack I had.

Trying to do too much and reluctant to designate to others. It was the old story; I'm quicker doing it myself rather than teaching others. I was only age 48. A heart attack! (and I had stopped smoking just one week before that!).

'Oh God' I thought, 'is this the end?'. I remember one old lady customer in the Ayr shop said to me "Ach a widnae worry son, I know someone that had a heart attack and lived for another 15 years".

'Well,' I thought, 'I'd settle for that... I'd be only two years short of normal retirement age... Aye I'll take it'.

This fright I got did give me a different outlook on the world. It emphasised what's really important in life and I made the changes that were required and stopped worrying about things that were outwith my control. So here I am, thirty years later and still looking for a few more years to come. That guardian angel, has sure been doing a good job with me, I'd recommend him! Or is it a 'her?'

I sold my Ayr post office in 1988 and went into semi-retirement.
The following year, at 50 years of age, Rena and I became grandparents for the first time with the birth of Maureen's son Jason.
This reminds me of another fright we got when Jason was about five years old. Maureen and the family were living halfway across the world in the Far East, in Borneo to be precise.
Jason was diagnosed with a life threatening condition and was flown to Singapore for treatment. It was a very worrying time but thankfully Jason overcame any problems and in 2014 provided us with our first Great Grandchild, Darcy.

Fairly soon thereafter, I was approached by a newspaper group based in Paisley who seemed keen to offer me the Group Advertisement Manger's post, which I did accept.
This small newspaper group was owned by 'United Newspapers', whose headquarters were at The Yorkshire Post offices, in Leeds.
After being involved in very successful local papers in Ayrshire, these titles in Paisley, Johnstone, Barrhead and Glasgow Southside were a very poor comparison and I really was not too happy there.
The Group however seemed to be satisfied with what I was doing and soon appointed me onto the local Board of Directors in the Paisley area.

Q96 RADIO STATION IN PAISLEY

I only spent two or three years with the Paisley Newspaper but one or two members of staff, including the then chairman, were involved in preparing an application for a local radio licence for Paisley.
They approached me to ask if I would be interested in becoming the general manager and also be responsible for advertising sales and administration, in the event that they were to be successful in their application. I accepted their offer and in due course the consortium were granted the licence from the Independent Broadcasting Authority and I moved there in 1992 as Director and Manager of Q96 Local Radio

Station.

Now, advertising sales, promotions, administration, sales teams and man management are qualities that I possess at very high standards. Well, that's what I am saying, blowing my own trumpet, anyway who can argue with that, my record in local newspapers is legend. Big heid!

I did arrange many press releases, for local and Scottish newspapers, for the launch of Q96 and I was featured in a number of publications. Not all of it was welcome as local newspapers were in competition for the Paisley advertisers £.

Radio, however, is just not my forte. I knew, and still know, absolutely nothing about music. Unless it is music from the 1950s, I just don't have a clue. So on the broadcasting side it was left to proper 'radio men', and to be honest I was a fish out of water in that environment. The selling techniques of radio advertising is totally different from newspapers, and whilst I was uncomfortable with it, we were as successful as could be reasonably expected, being so close to the highly successful 'Radio Clyde'.

I was involved in a lot of the initial publicity and promotions to launch the radio station and we commissioned the popular band Hue and Cry for a promotion in the town centre of Paisley.

After about 3 years, Q96 Radio Station was acquired by a new consortium and many changes were effected.

New personnel were introduced and a new advertising whizz kid, at enormous expense, was supposed to increase the advertising revenue. The desired results did not materialise, in fact he didn't do as well as my results... without the extra expense.

In 1996, therefore I approached the company suggesting that it would be in everyone's interest if I were offered a redundancy package. That scenario came to pass and quite frankly I was happy to be out of that, for me, completely unsuitable environment.

I wasn't quite 60 so I was too young to just sit with my feet up.

SELLING DOOR TO DOOR

At that time the Government was anxious to bring competition into the energy fuel market. I got a freelance job, on commission only, with SSEB going round doors encouraging people to save on their gas bills by changing to SSEB and thereby ensuring smaller bills.

For a salesman, selling a service for which there is no charge and resulting in savings for the customer, it's a no brainer. Any salesman worth his salt should be highly successful. At the interview, I asked what was the target number of contracts to be signed daily and was told 5. I realised later that the average results by their sales force was in fact less than that. I only worked Monday to Friday from about 2pm until about 6pm knocking on doors in the Erskine area initially and on my first day I did get the target of five contracts.

Thereafter, I never got less than 10 on any day's work and more often I got 12, 13 or 14. My average over the first few weeks was actually 13 and the highest I got in one day was 15. When I reached the 13 mark, I often would call it a day and make my way home.

This was the only occupation I ever had which involved door to door selling and it really is an experience. Not least by the number of dogs that always seemed to have a desire to maul me.

"It'll no touch you son, it's just being friendly". Well it could sure fool me.

German shepherd breeds were my greatest fear and I probably lost a few sales due to my canine friends. When the door was answered and you were invited in, you just didn't know what to expect regarding the state of the home and often you wished immediately that you hadn't knocked that door. The rancid odour, often mixed with a tobacco smell, almost made you boke. It is truly incredible to think of the mire and filth that some people are living in. I am not talking of poverty, I mean just sheer laziness, lack of self-esteem and acceptance to live, eat and sleep in such squalor is really very sad.

"Would you like a wee cup of tea, I've just got the kettle on".

Dear God, if I lived in that house I would die of malnutrition.

"Naw thanks, I've just had one ten minutes ago".

I only spent a few months doing this job and left it as the cold winter months came on.

The agency handling SSEB contacted me later offering me a supervisor position in their showrooms. Training and supervising the 'commission only' staff, who were doing the same job as I did door to door, with the customers coming into the showrooms.

It was then that I realised how poor some people are at selling. Many were only capable of achieving one or two contracts per day and some days none at all. I spent a few hours one day with a saleswoman and we got 10 contracts signed that day. Hopefully, I thought, she has learned something today and I was anxious to see her results the following day. Zero, zilch, was her total. I couldn't continue doing this job with people who just didn't have it, so it did not last too long.

A friend of mine, who had been the editor at one of the local newspapers we both used to work for, had a contract to produce and edit a publicly funded publication in Drumchapel every 2 months.

He suggested to them that they could help fund the publication by selling advertising space to local traders and businesses...

"And I know someone who could handle that very capably, on a commission only basis".

He was of course referring to me and it came to pass that I was given that task. It proved to be very profitable for the Association and also for me.

This project lasted for about three or four years until they wanted to bring the issues out every month. The monthly frequency did not suit me. I had been approached to do a similar job with another publicly funded newspaper in Lanarkshire, not only the advertising side but also set the copy and compile the 'print ready' news pages.

This newspaper was issued quarterly and this suited me fine. They then increased it by doing the same thing for two additional areas, so I had three issues at the same time every three months.

There was a short period when I was handling both the Drumchapel newspaper advertising and the Lanarkshire publications, so I was happy to lose the Drumchapel issue.

It was around this time that we started holidaying and eventually spending winters in Florida, so the benefits of retirement began to take precedence over employment. When I finally stopped working with the last newspapers that I was involved with, I was approaching my mid seventies, so at that age I think I deserved a rest.

SENIORS IN THE SUNSHINE STATE

In the early part of this millennium, Rena and I were both retired and started going on holiday to Florida, to the Gulf Coast in the Tampa Bay area. We became very attached to this part of the 'Sunshine State', probably because it was always in a state of sunshine.

We were very impressed with the 'senior living' communities of mobile and manufactured homes and the wonderful facilities and activities on offer at these parks.

After a couple of years, we decided to purchase a mobile home in a community called Westwind in Dunedin, a wonderful little town on the coast, about 7 miles from Clearwater.

When I say it was a 'mobile home', there was nothing mobile about it. The floor space measured about 1,400 square ft., there was a very large lounge, a conservatory, which is called a sun room over there, two bedrooms and walk-in closets, two bathrooms with shower or bath, a large kitchen and an outside shed with washer and dryer.

It was unbelievably cheap in comparison to homes in Scotland so we thought it might be an investment for holidays for 3 or 4 years till we got fed-up with it. Well, we really fell in love with the home, the community, and the whole 'snowbirds' concept.

Hundreds of thousands of retired and semi retired Canadians and Americans from the colder states, spend their winters in communities like ours throughout Florida. These people are called 'snowbirds'.

It wasn't just Rena and I, all our children and grandchildren absolutely loved holidaying in our Dunedin home and they were regular visitors. The improvements I made to our home included installing double glazed windows throughout, new carpeting, new bathrooms and kitchen with new appliances and tiled floors. Totally covered the exterior with vinyl siding and had a new fully insulated roof-over applied. I did all this work myself or with Gerard, our son, except the roof over which was a specialised operation.

Over the first 2 or 3 years I added an additional room, which Gerard and I built and then I erected a closed in patio at the rear of the house. The property could actually sleep 8 in beds and sofa beds, and the sunroom could also take another two people. So it could sleep 10 comfortably in 5 separate sleeping rooms – mobile home? – you must be joking!

When we had been there about two years, we decided to have all the floors re-carpeted with a nice beige coloured carpet throughout the home. The carpet fitters arrived and to our amazement rolled out the carpet on the roadway to cut it as required.

There is no way this job could have been done inside without great difficulty and danger of error. Anyway, it was a lovely sunny day, dry and warm, and I controlled any traffic that attempted to use the road. We just cannot imagine carpet fitters doing this in 'sunny' Scotland but it certainly made the fitters job a lot easier.

We bought a lovely old Buick Le Sabre saloon car, which transported us all over Florida and later upgraded to a Mercury Sable. I loved both of those cars.

The Westwind Community Park is owned by the residents and everyone had the option to buy a share, which we did after three years.

That meant I was eligible to be voted on to the Board of Directors, which occurred soon after.

I then convinced the board and the residents that we should have a website, which I produced and maintained as Webmaster. If you google; westwindresidentownedcommunity.com and browse through the pages you will see how attractive the Westwind Park is.

I said we intended to spend 3 or 4 winters there but that extended to 12 years, the main reason we sold up was due to me needing some attention to my heart problems.

I had a heart attack 30 years earlier and so our holiday insurance did not cover the dreaded 'pre-existing conditions', so I was not covered for anything connected to the heart condition.

If I had to pay for hospitalisation or treatment in the USA I would have been bankrupt, so we thought we better not take unnecessary risks.

Although we left the community, I still continued to maintain the website.

Whilst in Florida, I was much more sporty and agile than at home and participated in activities such as, golf, cycling, walking, ten-pin bowling and shuffleboard. Our social life was more active too, with street parties, dances, concerts, beach picnics and lots of games.

I also got some lessons in stained glasswork and produced some nice items. My very first attempt was two windows (approximately 30 inches x 40 inches each), situated between our lounge and sunroom. I drew a design which was intended to be in the Charles Rennie Mackintosh style and featured the 'Glasgow Rose', or at least my attempt at it. I was indeed very proud of my first effort at stained glass work. A photograph is shown in the centre section of the book.

My second venture in glasswork was a welcome sign and when completed I enclosed it in a light box which I constructed. Each year, I would erect it outside our door and when the neighbours and walkers in the park saw it illuminated they knew we were back in Florida for the winter.

A TASTE OF SCOTLAND

Two of our Florida highlights were featured one year apart.

I had got heavily involved in the social events at the two clubhouses in the community and I wanted to put on an event to give the residents a wee experience of Scotland, so I organised a 'Taste of Scotland' night.

I gave a prolonged talk aided by photo slide shows and videos emphasising the beauty of Scotland.

The Americans were thrilled with all the castles and stately homes and the history, but I also focused attention on the many inventions, discoveries and contributions that the Scots have given to the world.

In addition, with a little help from some Scottish volunteers in the community, I provided traditional Scottish fare - haggis, neeps and tatties, oatcakes and cheddar, Scottish trifle and tablet.

Naturally there was whisky sampling plus some beers and soft drinks. Unfortunately, America does not allow the import of Irn Bru so our other national drink was not sampled.

The hall that night was packed to capacity and there were a number of disappointed people who didn't manage to get a ticket. There was no cover charge and whilst I got an Irish whisky company to provide me with whisky and Kerrygold to supply me with cheese and butter, buying the other drinks and foods probably set me back about $250. We wanted to give something back to the community in return for the enjoyment we got from living in this winter paradise.

The Scottish night was such a success that they pleaded with me to do a 'Taste of Ireland' night the following year.

That event followed along the same lines as the Scottish night and once again 'The Irishman' whiskey and 'The Irish Cream' was kindly provided. On the food line we had Irish soda bread, Irish cheese, scones with cream and jam.

The slide shows and videos covered the beauty of Ireland plus Irish myths and legends, Riverdance and much more.

On this occasion there was a nominal charge for a ticket, (which included a free prize draw), or a donation. All monies collected went to the charity 'Mary's Meals' and I raised over $600 for this great cause. The hall once again was filled to capacity and the night was again voted a huge success.

We were only about a 45 minute drive from Busch Gardens in Tampa and we took advantage of the great offers of annual season tickets for

Florida residents which was very little more than the cost of a one day entry ticket.

This allowed us to attend the theme park and be entertained with shows featuring some artists of yesteryear. We regularly attended concerts with the likes of, the Big Band sounds of Glen Miller and Tommy Dorsey. The Osmonds, The Four Aces, Peter Noone and Hermans Hermits, The Platters, The Drifters, Debbie Reynolds and so many more. We even got a reduction for food in the restaurants and 10% off all shop purchases. The gardens and the animals at the theme park were a delight, so we rarely took advantage of the roller coasters and countless other rides.

Their seasonal stage shows at Christmas and the Ice shows were super and they did special shows for Halloween and other events.

Yes we did have 12 wonderful winters in Dunedin, in the sun.

SONGS FROM THE HEART

For the first three or four years of spending the winter months in Florida we would fly home for the festive period, we naturally wanted to be with the family at Christmas.

We discovered however that the cruise lines offered exceptionally cheap fares on the transatlantic crossing on their repositioning cruises, so we weighed up the cost of two return flights against one cruise out about October and one back around April. There was little difference in cost but on each cruise we had an all-inclusive, 2-week, luxury holiday on board with all you could eat and lots of free entertainment. It was a no-brainer.

It meant of course that we would not be with the family over Christmas and that was a bit hard to take.

I think it was on the second or third occasion of us being in Florida over Christmas that the family, our children and grandchildren, gave us the most wonderful and treasured Christmas gift that any parents could receive.

Our son Gerard made a short visit to us a few weeks before Christmas and left a parcel filled with presents that had not to be opened until

Christmas Day.

In a phone conversation with Frances Marie she whispered to me that we would be very pleased with the joint family Christmas present that we were to receive, but gave no indication of what it could be.

The big day arrived and we opened the box of presents. One, marked from all the family, was a CD, entitled 'Songs From The Heart'

It was sealed in cellophane paper and had a professional looking CD cover so to all intents and purposes it looked to us that they had bought us a CD… That puzzled me… a CD as our special present?

We opened it and were amazed at the information on the cover and the inside, the artwork was truly professional, the recordings were made in a 'studio' at Frances Marie's home, the music was, in the main by Scott who, with Gerard, was also responsible for the recording.

Each member of the family sang a song or more than one, there were some songs sang by all of them and even one, which was a recording of me singing 'Old Maid in the Garret' but they edited it adding the whole choir joining me in the last verse and chorus.

Rena and me listened to each of the sixteen tracks, blinded in tears, especially the last two numbers; Frances Marie singing 'Medals for Mothers' and Gerard singing 'The Old Man'

Frances Marie was correct, this WAS the most treasured Christmas gift we have ever received. I still shed a tear when I listen to 'The Old Man'…ach I'm a sentimental old fool!

ANECDOTES & AXED-TOES

UNCLE JOE'S TOES

My father's brother, my Uncle Joe...well actually his name was in fact Patrick, but he was always known as, and went under the name of Joe, but officially he was Patrick.

Now, this may have been because in the very early 20th century in the West of Scotland, it may have been easier to get a job if your name was not Patrick. Whatever the reason, our family only ever knew him as Uncle Joe although we did hear some talk of the name Patrick.

Uncle Joe was the youngest of our father's family and worked for my father in some of his cobbler shops. Later in life he had a cobbler shop of his own in Cairnhill, Airdrie.

Joe was quite a gentle soul and he had a very dry sense of humour. He could tell a story and maintain a deadpan expression on his face, which made the listeners believe every word he spoke.

He always cracked a joke and had a wry smile on his face. He and his wife, our Aunt Lizzie, had eight children and most of our family had one of these cousins in the same class, or next class at the primary school.

Joe did have some kind of medical ailment with his feet, and apparently, it was quite a serious complaint inasmuch the condition actually meant that some of his toes had to be amputated.

We would hear stories that "Uncle Joe has had to get another toe removed". This seemed to happen so many times over the years that, sarcastic comments were being made about how many toes he must have had to start with, if he has had so many removed.

Uncle Joe, however, lived into his nineties and near the end this problem with his feet had spread into the legs or leg.

He also maintained his humour and joviality right to the end, as his son Vincent explained to us when we attended the wake.

He was in a ward at Monklands hospital in Airdrie and there was nothing they could do for the condition and it was decided that one of his legs would require to be amputated.

Vincent said, "When I visited the hospital about ten days ago, the nurse drew me aside and said she was concerned that my dad might be losing his mind".

She said "When we told him that he may have to have his leg amputated he just looked at me, with just the hint of a slightly puzzled face, and said to me… does this mean that I'll have a limp hen?"

Vincent knew of course that his father was well aware of the situation, but true to his habit of a lifetime and using his deadpan expression, he tried to make a joke out of a serious situation.

One of my nephews, and Uncle Joe's great nephew, Fr. Jim Grant, who is a priest, went to visit Uncle Joe at Monklands hospital.

He enquired at the reception as to which ward Joe was in and after some searching the receptionist said "Sorry Father, there isn't any Joseph Grant in any of the wards"

Fr. Jim said, "Well I'm quite sure he is in the hospital somewhere, could you have another wee check please?"

The receptionist duly checked again and said the only male Grant is a Patrick Grant.

Now that must have rung a bell with Jim and he said to the receptionist, "do you happen to know how many toes he has got?"

Fr. Jim celebrated the Requiem Mass at Joe's funeral and in his eulogy he reiterated the story of his visit to the hospital which brought a note of humour to the ceremony that, I have no doubt, would have met with Uncle Joe's approval.

DID I WITNESS TULLY'S FAMOUS DOUBLE?

My son Gerard, a few years ago, was collecting football match pro-grammes and other memorabilia. We were wintering in Florida at the time and he phoned me asking if I was at a Scottish Cup football match in 1953, at Brockville Park in Falkirk. He had acquired a book *(Celtic, A Complete Record 1888 – 1962)* and a page therein (see cen-tre photo section) featured the occasion when the famous Charlie Tul-ly, in a cup-tie against Falkirk, scored a goal direct from a corner kick without anyone else touching the ball. That is a very rare occurrence. Some crush barriers gave way and fans were on the pitch. The referee however, for some reason disallowed the goal and ordered the corner kick to be retaken. Charlie, incredibly, repeated his feat and this time the goal stood. This page of the aforementioned book was covering this historical event and there was a photograph of some fans with the caption; *'Celtic fans at Brockville in the 1950s. The crowd at the Scot-tish Cup tie there in 1953 saw a remarkable double strike by Charlie Tully'*

When Gerard asked me about being at the match I told him that I, in fact, had been at a Falkirk v Celtic cup-tie at Brockville in the early 1950s but I didn't think I was at the match where Charlie scored his famous double. An event like that should be easily remembered, but I do remember crush barriers giving way and being pushed onto the pitch, so perhaps that dulled my memory a bit.

Gerard and his sisters were debating whether I was one of the fans in the photograph. I told them that whilst at the match in Falkirk, a pho-tographer from the national photojournalistic magazine *'The Picture Post'* did take a snap of the fans around me. I never saw any photo published but that's not surprising because it was a publication that we did not buy although it had a weekly circulation of over 1.5 mil-lion, so whether it ever appeared in the *Picture Post*, I never did know.

He emailed me the photo and it most definitely was myself in the photograph. I remember being there and also the crowd barriers breaking and fans spilling on to the pitch. I checked records and it turns out that in 1953 and 1954 Celtic played Falkirk in the Scottish Cup at Brockville, so perhaps this photo was taken in 1954. I'm afraid I cannot state categorically which year.

In the photograph, I am the handsome young lad, bottom left, with the rosette. If it was 1953 I was 14 years old and if it was 1954 I was 15. So which year do you think it was?

I have had further thoughts on this. On checking records, the 1954 game was on a Wednesday afternoon and on that date, I had recently started in my very first job. I would have been working on a Wednesday so perhaps it was the 1953 game and I was on the pitch when the barriers collapsed in front of me. I would have been more concerned about my safety rather than who scored the goal.

AN AVERSION TO AIR TRAVEL

It is fair to say that I am not a great fan of air travel, even though at age 8 or 9, my sister Mary Therese and her then fiancé (not a word we used much in the early 40s), Arthur Brannigan, took me on a pleasure flight on a small double winger aircraft at Prestwick Airport. At that time it was bragging material with all my schoolmates and made them really jealous.

My dislike of air travel is an underlying fear of something technically going wrong.

If your car breaks down you just get out and walk. If you are on a cruise and you hit an iceberg, there are more than sufficient lifeboats to rescue you and there's always the lifebelts.

With a serious fault on an aircraft, electrical or otherwise, gravity takes over and from 20,000ft it's curtains for everyone.

We depend on all the engineers and technicians doing their job meticulously and air traffic controllers not going to sleep on the job. In addition to that, we now have the fear of terrorist involvement to be concerned with.

How a jumbo jet with all its passengers and luggage and weighing probably over 300,000 kilograms can defy gravity after only a short drive along a runway, will always be beyond my comprehension. Yet, I put all my trust in something I don't understand.

You may be wondering why I am rabbiting on about flying, or fear of, but it will be clearer shortly.

Rena and I decided in 2007 that we would have a 'once in a lifetime' holiday for all the family, our children and spouses and our six grand-children.

We had, by that time, started to cross the Atlantic to and from our winter home in Dunedin, Florida, by sailing on beautiful cruise ships. These were known as repositioning cruises lasting 13 or 14 nights and they were really good value for money, most of them less than half the price a cruise of that duration would cost. Going to Florida around October or November and sailing back around April or May, there were usually a number of cruise lines to choose from. We had recently sailed on Royal Caribbean's *'Navigator of the Seas'*, a new addition to their fleet.

Our plan was to fly our family out on the *Globespan Airline* a few days before Christmas 2007, from Glasgow to Sanford, Orlando. Hire two 8 seater people carriers and then drive to our home in the wonderful Community Park in Dunedin, just a few miles from Clearwater in the Tampa Bay area.

We arranged for all the family to be accommodated in a few of our friend's homes. In fact our next door neighbour, Helen, was going back to Boston for Christmas and insisted that we take the keys for her home and for her car for the duration of the holiday. Yes, we had wonderful neighbours.

We also booked the family on a 5 night Christmas cruise on *'The Nav-igator of the Seas'* from Miami to the Caribbean islands and Cozumel in Mexico.

After that, booked a hotel in St Petersburg, (Florida, not Russia), for Hogmanay, then go back to Dunedin for a couple of days before flying home from Sanford.

This family holiday made a massive dent in our retirement savings, but it is one of the best things we have ever done because every last one of the family agreed it was the most fabulous experience of their lives.

For most of them, spending Christmas Day on the beach at Cozumel enjoying all the fabulous activities in which they participated, made this their most memorable Christmas ever.

When booking the air flights from Glasgow to Sanford, there was a change of dates for the flights from Glasgow and our daughter Maureen couldn't get the outward date holiday from work, so she went via Newark with a different airline.

All the remaining members of the family flew to and from Sanford together.

At the end of the holiday the two hired vehicles were returned at the airport and Rena and I travelled in our car to see them all off on the plane.

We said our goodbyes and they all climbed the stairs to go through security and we could see them through the glass partition as they slowly moved on. We, and they, were waving to each other all the time and there were tears in both our eyes. Not just because we were parting, but because it dawned on me that …Oh God, I cannot bear to think.

This horrifying thought was going through my mind. Is this the last time Rena and I will see our children and grandchildren? If that plane goes down our family is wiped out, except for one daughter and she would have lost her two sons on that plane too.

I was actually trembling at the thought and promised myself that I would never have the situation again that all the family eggs are in the same basket, so to speak.

The last of them waved goodbye and I don't even know who it was, the tears blinded me, I could just see a waving hand.

We then made our way to the car to drive the 90 minutes home to

Dunedin, with a somewhat heavy heart.

"Have faith in God" said Rena "they'll get home safe" as she often said when I seemed to lack confidence in a desired outcome.

We were back in our Dunedin home and having a tea and coffee before getting ready for bed.

"They'll be almost two hours into their journey" Rena said.

A little while later the telephone rang and I was surprised and bewildered, in fact shocked, to hear the voice of our youngest daughter Catriona. She should have been in the air these last three hours... we saw them heading for the boarding gate... and the flight was 'on time'.

My first thought was *'Good God, you are supposed to be on that plane, what the hell has happened?'*, then I thought the plane must have has been delayed, well, these things happen, it's a bit of a nuisance but so be it.

Catriona then told us exactly what happened.

"Not long after take off we had settled down for the journey then we all heard a massive bang... it was terrifying, I was at a window seat near the wing and looking out I could see flames coming from one of the engines."

"Many of us started panicking, the captain announced to the passengers that there was a problem with one of the engines ... we all, were very aware of that".

"He said that we could continue to Glasgow on one engine but he had decided to dump the fuel and return to Sanford Airport".

I'm sure all on board agreed emphatically with that decision.

Catriona went on to tell us about everyone's reaction, who panicked most (I think it was herself) and how petrified everyone was in the short journey back to Sanford.

The runway was sprayed with foam for an emergency landing, but thankfully the aircraft landed successfully.

All the passengers were then accommodated at an airport hotel overnight and told that a replacement plane would leave early next morning.

The initial shock and horror of hearing her story turned to relief when she confirmed that everyone was OK, there were no injuries to anyone on board.

Rena and I immediately got back into the car and set off on the two-hour drive headed for their hotel in Sanford.

We didn't book in, we just all shared rooms, I don't think anyone slept very soundly that night anyway.

It was early morning when all those for the flight boarded a bus for the airport. We didn't go back to the airport, we just drove home to Dunedin.

My mind was not at rest until we got phone calls from Scotland that everyone was safely back home, Thank God.

Maureen, who had left for her flight to Newark much earlier than the others, was not aware of the traumatising experience until she got home.

Next day, on the internet, I read, in the Daily Record, the full press coverage with quotes and photographs of passengers involved in the incident.

Perhaps you will understand why I wish to reaffirm here, **I do not like flying!**

SHAFTED AT THE ABBEY

When I got home from National Service in 1960, my first 'holiday' was to spend a week doing volunteer labouring at the building of *Nunraw Abbey* near Haddington in East Lothian.

This was a project that was to take about 30 years so I wasn't sure if I would live to see the finished building but I did and visited it a few years ago.

My cousin Hugh McGoldrick, one of the few friends we had who owned a car, drove me to *Nunraw Abbey Guest House* in Garvald, East Lothian.

It was in this impressive towered building that we were fed each day with breakfast and a lunch. I think we paid about half a crown per day for food, which was also cooked by volunteer labour.

On arrival, I thought we would be staying in the guest-house which was very impressive indeed. No such luck, our accommodation was a former prisoner of war Nissan hut in Garvald (used for Italians I believe, during the war).

It was only one hut crammed with a number of metal bunk beds, each with a mattress and a blanket, no sheets as I recall... well we only slept there. We were transported to the Abbey by open lorries, I think they belonged to *Doonan Brothers* of Uddingston, but I may not have the right name.

We would buy a few cans of beer in the evening and spend the time singing a selection of Irish drinking songs and go to the building site next morning with a sore head.

On the building site, I was allocated the task of wheeling barrow loads of concrete up narrow planks of wood to a kind of platform, and then empty the concrete into ready made moulds of arches.

A barrow full of concrete is one helluva push up those planks and one was happy to dump that weight into the moulds.

Then we wheeled the empty barrow down two planks of wood to ground level about 6ft. below, putting the barrow wheel on one plank and my feet on the other.

With the constant bumping of the wheel on to one of the planks, it gradually edged ever closer to the edge of the platform and likewise the plank that supported your weight.

I think it was on the second day of working at the site and after a few trips up and down the ramps with the barrow, I stepped on one of the planks and it gave way. I then dropped down about 6feet onto broken bricks and rubble. But that was not the worst occurrence.

The barrow wheel was on the other plank so it didn't want to descend, so as I fell downwards still holding the tubular shaft of the barrow, that was the part that struck my chin making a huge gash one inch below my mouth.

Although I was bruised and sore by the fall on to the broken bricks, my concern was the damage caused by the metal shaft and the seemingly endless pouring of blood.

I was fortunate in a way that I was not struck one inch further up or I would have lost most, if not all, of my teeth.

One of the monks took me by car to Haddington Hospital and I think I had about 6 or 8 stitches on my chin. The scar of that attack by the handle of the barrow stayed with me for the rest of my life, but it has gradually became less conspicuous.

For a while thereafter, if someone asked about the scar, I would say… "I got that in a monastery… a mad monk attacked me".

OUR FIRST HOME

We were married in 1963 and lived first of all in a room in my mother's house and then in Rena's mother's house, so as you can imagine we were desperate for a place of our own. It would need to be a place to rent because there was no way we could afford to buy a home then and the chance of a Local Authority house was way down the road.

I was working with *British Transport Advertising* selling advertising spaces on railway properties and on buses, more commonly on buses. I had a very large area to cover in the West of Scotland, from Dumfriesshire up to Glasgow. This included Ayrshire, Renfrewshire and half of Glasgow.

In the course of this job, I would visit some towns and areas for the first time. I was in the habit, at lunchtimes, of visiting the local Catholic Church to say a wee prayer. Now there is an old Catholic belief that when you visit a church for the very first time and spend a little time in prayer, you can make a wish, not that I believed in such superstitions, but… well... you never know!

The first time I visited the Royal Burgh of Irvine, before it became a new town, it was a lovely, warm and sunny day.

I crossed over the old bridge across the river Irvine and looked down on the beautiful Low Green on the riverbank. I just fell in love with the place, it was so different from gloomy Lanarkshire. I visited St Mary's church in West Road and felt totally at home therein. I remembered the old saying about getting a wish, so I made it clear, to whichever celestial angel or saint that was listening to my prayer, that

I wanted a house in this town.

Shortly after that I was in Ayr with the proof of an advert for a carpet shop, which was to appear on buses in the Ayr depot.

The owner of the shop wasn't in, but I spoke with his assistant Jimmy Alexander who said that he would possibly be interested in advertising on the buses, as he was soon to take possession of premises in Irvine for a carpet shop. When he mentioned Irvine my ears cocked up. I related that I just fell in love with that town and would love to live there.

"Well this shop I'm moving into has a room and kitchen attached to it, so it could be available for rent".

My eyes lit up. "I would certainly be interested", I said.

"The only thing is", he continued, "my son is getting married and he may want to move in there".

'Aw shit' I thought, 'he's building me up to let me down'.

"Oh, well here's my card, if by any chance it becomes available, I'd appreciate being considered as a tenant"

He said he would, but I thought, ach, it's too good to be true.

A couple of weeks later, on a Thursday, I got a phone-call at the office… "Its Jimmy Alexander here, you said you could be interested in this room and kitchen that I've got".

Rena and I went down there on the Saturday, negotiated a rent of £1 per week, and moved in the following Saturday with our one year old son Gerard. We had a house of our own at last and by the seaside too. So that's how we came to live in Ayrshire.

We bought a second hand washing machine soon after that and installed it in the crammed kitchen.

All the electric sockets in the house were 5amp, not really suitable for washing machines. Often, when it was turned on, it fused the electric box in the whole building and his carpet shop would be in darkness.

I remember Jimmy would go berserk, stomp up the entry lobby shouting, "Have you got that bloody washing machine on again, all the lights are out"

Anyway, he did not evict us and we spent three happy years in that house adding two more children, two daughters, Maureen and Frances Marie, both born in the same year, Frances Marie making it into 1966 by just three days.

It was shortly after Frances Marie was born that we got on the property ladder with our first home in Mill Road, Irvine. The 3 bedroom semi-detached *McTaggart & Mickel* house cost £4,000, a large sum of money in 1968.

Some of my siblings were very concerned that we had 'put a millstone round our neck' taking out a mortgage for that amount of money. Oh, how wrong they were, but, if I'm honest, I was just a little bit apprehensive too at the beginning.

Our back garden area in Mill Road backed on to the very large gardens of the local authority houses in Clark Drive, which were mostly occupied by very elderly residents who no longer were fit to do gardening. One of them had a half derelict greenhouse.

Around this time, Rena was working part-time as a nurse in Kilmarnock Infirmary, night shift on Fridays, Saturdays and Sundays. I therefore had the four children to look after at the weekend so I began to get interested in gardening and growing vegetables.

I spoke to the elderly Clark Drive residents and asked if I could use their garden areas for sowing potatoes etc. They agreed and I also had the use of the greenhouse. I became almost obsessed with gardening and I was aided by the exceptional quality of the soil, everything I grew, without any fertiliser I may add, turned out to be wonderful.

I grew tomatoes and cucumber in the greenhouse and even entered my 'long green ridge' cucumbers in the Ayr Flower Show at which they won first prize. They were huge and I remember at the flower show, when I was gazing at the 'winner ticket', a lady asked me "how do you cook marrows, son?" … that's how big they were.

My brother-in-law Arthur, whose pet food hate is cucumber, could actually eat my cucumber and said they tasted more like water-melon… praise indeed.

I grew lots of potatoes, but also cabbage, brussel sprouts, beetroot, carrots, leeks, onions and of course lettuce. I also had a large strawberry patch.

The elderly neighbours were well supplied with the produce I had grown, so also were many of our relations and even my work colleagues. I was truly a little market gardener but all produce was free to all recipients.

It was very rewarding to go out on a Sunday morning and dig up some potatoes, carrot, onions etc. for the Sunday dinner. Our daughter Maureen, however, was not too pleased with the potatoes, she wanted the 'real' potatoes from the shops, that weren't covered in dirt!

Millennium Greetings Cards

In 1999 as the new Millennium was approaching, I was retired, but the entrepreneur within me got to thinking, *'there must be some opportunity out there to make a buck or two'.*

I was going along the lines of old Scottish customs at Hogmanay, first-footing, 'lang may yer lum reek', lump of coal etc.

After a lot of thought I came up with the idea of a 'Millennium' greetings card and I went ahead and arranged to have 10,000 printed.

I have illustrated the card in the photo section but I must explain some of what was involved in the production of the cards.

I produced artwork of a fireplace based on the one in our lounge. There was a cut out on the card for the fire and a small piece of coal stuck to the inside of the card protruding through the front.

Above the fireplace there was an illustration of a mirror with a silver sticker with the words,

'Lang May Yer Lum Reek ... Happy New Millennium'.

On the inside (left) of the card it read:

A Scottish Ne'erday Custom

An old Scottish tradition on Hogmanay was, for those who were 'first-footing' their friends, to give them a piece of coal with the greeting 'Lang May yer Lum Reek'. A wish that they will have good fortune throughout the year and a cosy fire to welcome friends.

And on the right-hand side, a wee poem and Millennium greetings:

Frae a Scottish mine, sae dark and deep
Came this wee bit coal, noo sent tae you
A guid Scots custom, thereby we keep
Though cosy ingles noo, are few
But the New Year greeting, disnae vary
It's still the same, as aye it's been
Lang May Yer Lum Reek, warm and cheery
As this new Milllennium, comes oan the scene
Wishing you good health and prosperity
in the New Millennium

As I was hoping to sell these through retail shops and wholesalers, I had to apply for a bar code and get it printed on the back of the card.
I had a good relationship with a printer who printed the cards and made the necessary cut for the fire nest.
When I received the print job there was a number of procedures to be carried out:
The cut-out part had to be removed.
The silver stickers for the mirror had to be affixed (very precisely).
A small piece of coal had to be attached with double sided sticky pads.
The card was then folded and inserted in a plastic bag, also enclosing the envelope.
Packs of six cards were put in a plastic bag and sealed with a heat machine.
The cards then placed in cardboard boxes for transporting.

The biggest job was the gathering of 10,000 small pieces of coal (and getting them washed). This was very time consuming but we managed it. I personally carried out this task of the operation and Rena was in charge of the washing part.
Our games room with the full size snooker table became our produc-

tion factory and all the family were part of the 'conveyor belt' operation for almost three months.

Apart from the cards, I also produced over 5,000 hessian bags (approx. 4"x5") each containing a lump of coal and tied with a card relating the same story of the Hogmanay tradition and the greeting.

The hessian was bought in rolls 4ft wide, so it had to be cut into squares, then using a sewing machine they were hemmed and sewn into bags. The lump of coal then inserted and the card attached with a hessian string.

I had decided that greetings card wholesalers would be my best outlet and I visited one or two. They were greatly impressed with the cards and said they could sell thousands of them but sadly all their Christmas wares were arranged at trade shows around February or March... I WAS TOO LATE!

It was August/September when I got the idea, so I missed the Millennium bus.

I had to become a travelling salesman again, going round shops seeking orders. I did produce a lot of point of sale posters and leaflets and I sent press releases to all the local papers and to *The Sunday Post* and the *Evening Times* amongst other publications. I still had some contacts in the press world and it paid off as I got good write-ups.

The response from the *Sunday Post* was phenomenal. I got hundreds of phone calls from all over Scotland, England and Ireland and I posted the orders to everyone and trusted that they would send me the money.

Not one purchaser defaulted on payment, in fact many of them ordered a further supply.

I got a surprise one morning when listening to Terry Wogan on *Radio 2*.

It was changeover time with Terry and Ken Bruce and as they normally do they had a wee blether. Someone had sent Ken one of my cards and he showed it to Terry.

They had a wee discussion about the card and the Scottish Hogmanay traditions. It seems Ken was very impressed with my Millennium greetings card.

It was a very busy but quite enjoyable exercise over 3 months, and indeed was quite profitable. The gamble paid off and the profits were shared with the family.

A year later I had so many requests from people who had bought them, to see if I was producing them again for Hogmanay.

I changed the greeting on the mirror above the fireplace to read *'Happy New Year'* instead of *'Happy New Millennium'* and similar appropriate changes inside the card.

Unexpectedly, a few hundred more cards were sold.

AN IMAGINATIVE MIND

I have always had an enquiring mind and in my fantasies I would love to have been an inventor.

I am also obsessed with quizzes, puzzles and IQ testers or any game or puzzle that is based on words.

Throughout the years, I have had many brainwaves but not followed them through and some of the things I thought of, I have seen come to fruition. For example, many years ago I thought that it would make more sense to turn sauce bottles upside down to be standing on their neck, thus allowing the sauce to be at the point of exit when you lift the bottle and avoid the shaking process, which often turns out messy. Some manufacturers do this now with sauce and mayonnaise etc.

My mother was not averse to having corn flakes in the evening and I also would enjoy them at that time of day. The thought came to me that Kellogs should encourage more sales by suggesting in their advertising that corn flakes are not just for breakfast time. Years after I thought of it they did actually advertise in that fashion.

When I published my free-sheet newspaper I used, as fillers, many of the word puzzles I produced and even contemplated producing and publishing a small monthly booklet of puzzles, mainly word based. There were about a dozen or so different kinds of puzzles and IQ testers to be included in the publication. I didn't follow through on that one… I may still try that yet!

The Channel 4 programme *'Countdown'* was one of my favourites and I hated missing even one episode, so I recorded the programme every day on the VCR
I would actually play along with the contestants marking the scores as if I was another player, probably about 70% of the time I would beat the other two.
It gave me a sense of achievement if I could get a nine-letter word, especially if Susie Dent, *'the Guardian of the Dictionary'*, didn't see it. There were very few occasions when that occurred.
The glamorous Carol Vorderman was a big attraction although Richard Whiteley's endless puns became a bit annoying.
I had the bright idea that I should consider applying to be a contestant and, as is my style, I sent an application to presenter Richard Whiteley at Countdown in the form of rhyming verse:

I am a Countdown addict, every day I need a 'shot'
If I miss a single programme, then 'Happy' I am not

So the VCR, you'll understand, plays a vital role
To ensure a show is never missed, that's my daily goal

But a TV transmitter fault, outwith my control entirely
Has, today, deprived me, of seeing Carol V. and Mr Whiteley

A day deprived of Richard, may not sound much fun
But then again, I was spared, another dreadful pun

A Carol VOID day however, sure upsets the lads
When they cannot get the show, and had to watch the 'Ads.'

On some very rare occasions, a nine-letter word I see
And twice before I've found them, when missed by 'G of D'

It makes me even prouder, when the numbers game I win
When Carol must have missed it, 'cos she had that extra gin

My wife collects rare teapots, it's almost an obsession
She'd love to own a 'Countdown' one, 't'would be her prized posses-
sion

So I'd truly love to have a go, on the best game show in the nation
So put my name upon your list, consider this my application.

I did get an audition, along with about 15 other applicants, in a hotel in Princes Street in Edinburgh. It took the form of an actual word game and a numbers game and I feel that, on another day, I could have done much better. Maybe I was a little nervous or I just had an off day. The outcome was that I was not selected to go forward on that occasion, "due to the very high standard of the Edinburgh audition", but I was advised to apply again at a later date when it would be very probable that I would be selected.

I did not re-apply, my ego was dented. Perhaps it was fortunate that I should be unnerved at the audition rather than be embarrassed on live TV.

THE HORSE RACING BOARD GAME

About 20 years ago, I devised a board game based on horse racing. *'A Day at the Racetrack'.*

I worked on it over a long period, years really, just like a hobby and gradually added to it and improved it.

It included betting slips, owner's prizes, steward judgement cards, and eight model horses with jockeys in their owner's colours, racing over a 12 furlong, mile and a half race.

The interesting aspect is that there is no dice involved as right from 'the off' each horse's move determines the next move.

When I felt that I had perfected it, I produced a prototype of the game and of the box containing all the relevant pieces and money etc.

The rules of the game were printed and copyrighted. Separate rules included for the simpler game without the betting element, intended for younger persons.

There are literally thousands of permutations of which horse could win the race, so no one could anticipate the winner.

There can be up to eight players (horse owners) and there will be one person acting as banker, dealing with the betting slips and the payouts to the winners.

The stewards judgement cards can advance or recede one, or all, of the horses in the race.

Each player is issued with a certain amount of cash and decide for themselves which horses to bet on and how much to gamble.The game and the box are illustrated on the photo pages at the centre of the book.

As a family we have many times played the game, especially on occasions when we are hosting some guests.

Everyone who plays the game thinks it is indeed very exciting and they always suggest that I should pursue the project and get it into production or through some board game manufacturer.

Naturally, I always agree with them but I have never really followed through or investigated to see if there is any real potential in the game.

Perhaps I am not hungry enough… a hungry salesman is a good salesman.

A board game such as this cannot be patented as an invention, so the only way to protect it is to have the design registered with The UK Intellectual Property Office.

It's a complicated application supported with many photographs and I applied for registration of my design. It was granted and I received the authorised Certificate of Registration of a design to a board game. This licence lasts initially for 5 years and I have renewed it twice when each 5 year period expired because I'd hate it if some entrepreneur stole my idea.

Maybe some day, if I need the money, I may seek to get it on the market or maybe one of my children or grandchildren will do so when board games become popular again and can compete with the modern electronic games.

ARTISTIC AND MUSICAL TALENT? - IT'S IN THE GENES

A good upbringing, good example and a good education are the basis of personal success but perhaps there is also a modicum of hereditary talent that contributes to a degree. Maybe it's in the genes.

My Grandfather, I was told, although a manual worker in an iron works, dabbled a bit in poetry and perhaps that is whom I got my 'rhyming verse' habit from.

In my generation - of my brothers, Joe played with *Rawyards Silver Band*, John, however, was the only one seriously interested in music and he played guitar, banjo, mandolin, tin-whistle and latterly made and played dulcimers. John also was the singer in the family, although we all participated in the many regular family gatherings in all of our homes.

Of the next generation, (our children and my many nephews and nieces) there was only one, Jim Brannigan, who could be described as a musician. He made a living from being a folk singer in Canada.

It's a totally different story with the following generation, the Grant and Brannigan grandchildren. We affectionately refer to them with the collective noun -'The Brannigrants'. John's grandchildren, in addition to some of them being good vocalists, can give professional performances with instruments including, harp, guitar, banjo, bodhran, dulcimer and tin whistle. They all credit their grandfather John as being their inspiration. If only he had lived to witness the success of their music, singing and Irish dancing, his heart would burst with pride.

Almost all of his grandchildren participated and competed for many years in the annual 'Fleadh Cheoil', the Irish Festival of Music and most of them achieved some awards.

Music is a major part of their lives and apart from regularly playing at various venues in Glasgow, some have completed tours in Europe and America.

I said earlier that John actually made dulcimers and was playing at the Civic Centre in Motherwell when he collapsed and died… playing his beloved music.

His youngest grandson Eamonn, as a child, excelled in competitions at the Fleadh in Ireland and went on to become, even at a young age, one of the foremost Bodhran players in the Celtic music community in Scotland and Ireland. He also has toured parts of Europe and America.

Apart from the music and singing abilities there are others in this generation of the family who excel at Irish dancing One of John's granddaughters Ciara Nugent has many medals to verify her ability although she will admit that her cousin Laura Davidson, my sister's granddaughter, is at the top of that profession. Laura has been both junior and senior Scottish *'Irish Dance Champion'* and has taken part in World Finals representing Scotland. Sadly, just when she was due to go to the Montreal World Finals, Laura suffered an ankle break and had to pull out. She did make the finals the next year.

My grandson Scott Mitchell is a distinguished guitarist and plays in the band *'November Lights'* with singer/songwriter James Hopkins and three other members. Scott's brother Steven is indeed a very talented singer, he won the Ayrshire schools *'Young Singer of the Year'*. He did not, however, pursue a career using his singing talent and chose rather to enter the teaching profession.

It's not surprising therefore, that there have been very many 'music nights' at their mother's home with other talented close friends.

In the field of art there are two of my grandsons, Connor and Scott, who have produced amazing examples of their talent.

Connor, especially, has produced so many examples of his artistic skills. His sketches of many family members are greatly appreciated and the front cover of this book features his portrait of 'yours truly'.

After the death of Fr. Joe Brannigan, he sketched one of Joe from a photograph and surprised his great aunt Mary Therese by sending it in the post from Singapore, where he lives and works.

Although my sister, when she unexpectedly received the artwork, cried for a few days she was overwhelmed and delighted with the artwork and it is now framed and displayed in a commanding place in the hall of her home.

In his latest art project he creates bespoke images of a stag, the antlers designed in a Celtic knot and of a 'heilan coo' with the hair in Celtic design.

To accompany their talent, many of the 'Brannigrants' have also been gifted with remarkable beauty - and not just the boys!

It seems that brains and beauty go together in our family - Well I suppose I am a wee bit biased here.

It amazes me and makes me so proud when I read on Facebook of all their achievements.

I am also so very proud that so many of the Grant and Brannigan family have followed my wife Rena into the proud and caring profession of nursing, including our daughter Marie and granddaughter Lauren and Lauren's sister Monica is employed in Pharmaceuticals. I think at the last count there were about 17 nurses in the wider family connection.

So, I do believe there must be something in the genes that expresses itself so profoundly in so many of my mother's great grandchildren.

These were some of my recollections throughout my life but I have probably forgotten more than I remembered.

I hope I haven't bored you too much. Thank you for taking the time to read

THE END

Oh, one more wee story…

There was this Scotsman an Irishman and a German. They were all Heart Surgeons…

No… this is not the start of a joke … these wonderful professionals at The Golden Jubilee Hospital in Clydebank performed a very successful triple heart by-pass on me on 30th March 2017 and I am eternally grateful to them and to the wonderful and dedicated nursing staff who provided exceptional care of the highest quality.

Sincere thanks to all.

Some photos of me from the 1940s. I was the youngest in the family of six.
My brother Jim on the bike and as a National Service soldier in 1958.
Our wedding photo in 1963 and my father outside his cobbler shop on High Street, Airdrie

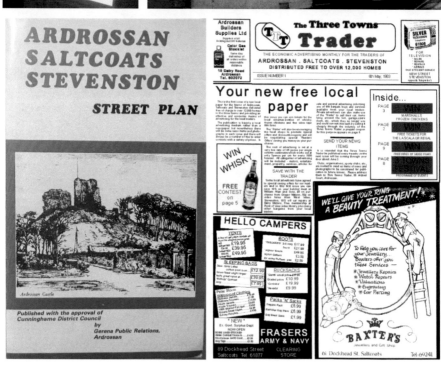

Some of my entrepreneurial projects;

The millennium Greetings cards.
My sub-post office and trophy business in Main Street Ayr.
The Street plan I published prior to introducing the free distribution advertising newspaper in Ardrossan, Saltcoats and Stevenston.

The Horse Racing board game I have devised and maybe some day will get it into production.
My first two ventures into stained glass work when in Florida and when the carpet fitters came
to renew the carpets at our Florida home they measured and cut the carpet on the road.
The CD recorded and produced by our children and grandchildren as a very special Christmas
present for Rena and I.

My class photo at St Margarets Airdrie in 1947.
Maurice Walsh, author of 'The Quiet Man' whom I met on the Dublin boat .
My mother's 10th birthday coincided with the visit to Airdrie of the King and Queen in 1914.
Wee Harry Roy who was seldom seen without his famous barrow.

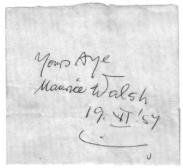